Twayne's English Authors Series

EDITOR OF THIS VOLUME

Kinley Roby

Northeastern University

Edwin Muir

TEAS 248

EDWIN MUIR

By ELGIN W. MELLOWN
Duke University

TWAYNE PUBLISHERS
A DIVISION OF G. K. HALL & CO., BOSTON

Published in 1979 by Twayne Publishers,
A Division of G. K. Hall & Co.
All Rights Reserved

Printed on permanent/durable acid-free paper and bound
in the United States of America

First Printing

Frontispiece of Edwin Muir is a
photograph made in London, July 1955,
by Mark Gerson FLIP. Reproduced
by permission.

Library of Congress Cataloging in Publication Data

Mellown, Elgin W
Edwin Muir.

(Twayne's English authors series ; TEAS 248)
Bibliography: p.
Includes index.
1. Muir, Edwin, 1887 - 1959—Criticism and
interpretation.
PR6025. U6Z77   828'.9'1209   78-15585
ISBN 0-8057-6687-1

Contents

About the Author

Elgin W. Mellown, a native of Alabama, received his B.A. from Emory University. After serving in the United States Army, he studied at Queen Mary College, University of London, where he received the M.A. in 1958, and at King's College, University of London, where he was awarded the Ph.D. in 1962. He has taught at the University of Alabama and is presently an Associate Professor of English at Duke University, Durham, North Carolina. He is the author of *Bibliography of the Writings of Edwin Muir* (University, Alabama: 1964; London: 1966), and, with Peter Hoy, of *A Checklist of Writings about Edwin Muir* (Troy, New York: 1971). In 1972 his *Descriptive Catalogue of the Bibliographies of Twentieth-Century British Writers* (Troy, N.Y.) was named by the American Library Association as one of the outstanding reference books of the year. The second, revised edition of this work was published in 1978 as *A Descriptive Catalogue of Twentieth-Century British Poets, Novelists, and Dramatists*. Dr. Mellown has published essays and reviews in many scholarly journals on topics ranging from Gerard Manley Hopkins' poems and their reception, to the novels of Jean Rhys, D. H. Lawrence, John Wain, Edwin Muir, and Laurence Sterne.

Preface

When Edwin Muir died in 1959, he was beginning to be recognized as a major poet, although he had long been known to an extremely large reading public as a literary critic, he and his wife, Willa, having early won international reputations as translators of significant German novels. Born on an Orkney tenant farm, he worked as a clerk in Glasgow before turning to journalism in 1919, and in the next forty years he established himself as a man of letters in both England and Scotland. In this study I survey his literary career, noticing almost everything that he wrote. Even though not all of his writings are equally valuable, I look at all of them for several reasons. His life and writings provide an instructive case history of the twentieth-century professional writer. There is also the fact that, lacking a formal education, Muir literally educated himself in public; and thus his reviews and other journalistic writings record his intellectual growth. But most important, his poems—which are his chief contribution to literature—are most easily understood in the light of his personal experiences and idiosyncratic philosophy, the latter being best explained in terms of his intellectual background.

For these reasons I employ the perhaps old-fashioned life-and-writings approach, not only because it allows one to come directly to the poet's work in verse and prose, but also because it is fairly close to Muir's own mature critical practice. I look at all of the writings while remaining constantly aware that the journalism, fiction, reviews, essays, biographies and autobiographies, travel books, and philosophical studies, interesting though they are in themselves, are read today because Muir is an important poet and must ultimately be seen as the background to and influence upon his poems.

I begin with a brief introductory chapter of biographical information which provides a chronological outline for the succeeding chapters, and which also points to some of the more significant events in the poet's life, the two most important being his marriage in 1919 to Willa Anderson (whose forceful personality so complemented Edwin's that it is impossible to think of the husband without thinking of the wife) and his realization in 1939 that he was a Christian. The next two chapters concern Muir's expository prose. I divide the enormous quantity of material surveyed here into professional journalism—book reviews, commissioned books on miscellaneous subjects, translations of German novels (there are well over thirty books in this category alone)—and into literary writings—essays and book-length studies on specifically literary topics. Some of these writings are still in print today; others were published and never reprinted; and all of them show Muir's intellectual growth and literary development.

The next chapter brings us closer to Edwin Muir the poet, for in it I examine his three novels and his two autobiographies, pointing out that the novels tell his personal story, even though they are set in widely differing times and places. Muir appears to have had much the same aim in writing fiction and verse, for during the years that he was writing fiction (roughly 1925 to 1931) he wrote very few poems; and later, when he was writing verse quite regularly, he wrote no fiction. The two autobiographies serve as glosses to the novels and to many of the poems; and it is actually possible to see one real experience of Edwin Muir in a prose version in his autobiography, in a prose account in one of his novels, and finally in a verse form.

The last three chapters are given over to a close study of Edwin Muir's poems, arranged chronologically. I look first at those verses composed in the 1920s and early 1930s when the poet was trying to gain the technical skill to express the difficult ideas that crowded in his mind and that he was discussing in his prose. The best poems of this early period are those in which Muir makes use of his intuitive recognition of archetypal symbols and mythic images, sources of poetry that can be recognized in all of his major poems. In the next chapter I examine those poems written just before Muir's important religious experience of 1939 and those which followed in the war years. In them we see the poet bringing his medium under control, for his religious experience appears to have released some block in his creative process and allowed the hiatus between thought and expression to be bridged. One of the important characteristics of Muir's middle period is a practice he may have learned from W. B. Yeats's collections of verse: to arrange the poems within each volume so that some poems are contradicted by those which surround them, while others are reinforced by the message of their neighbors.

This ability to appreciate individual poems as expressions of larger themes can be seen throughout the collections of the poet's last years, examined in the final chapter, for in these volumes Muir highlights the arrangement by the use of specific literary forms to mark turning points in his thought. The poems of this final period confirm the pattern of development that is apparent in the earlier years and establish Edwin Muir as the poet of traditional religious wisdom whose distinction lies in his use of psychologically valid symbols and in his artistic achievement within the bounds of a simple, direct language. Indeed, the simplicity of these late verses often makes them difficult to understand; but seeing them in the context of Muir's literary opus—and as the outgrowth of his life and works—we find a clear, unambiguous meaning in them. The poems of the late 1940s and 1950s give Muir a place in the tradition of such poets as Vaughan, Blake, and Wordsworth and show that his vision of life, like theirs, enabled him to see with "unblinded eyes . . . far and near the fields of Paradise."

ELGIN W. MELLOWN

Durham, North Carolina

Acknowledgments

My study of Edwin Muir's writings began shortly after the poet's death in 1959, and I incorporate in this book material from various essays and books on Muir which I published in the 1960s and 1970s. I have received (particularly in establishing the definitive bibliography of Muir's writings) help from so many people that, regretfully, I cannot name them all. I remember, however, with much gratitude the assistance which Willa Muir gave me, answering my questions in interviews and in letters. I should like also to express my thanks to Professor Geoffrey Bullough, now Professor Emeritus of London University, for his always helpful advice and for his friendship; and to Mr. Peter Hoy, Lecturer in French at Merton College Oxford, who has made significant additions to my bibliography of Muir's writings and who has collaborated with me in listing the secondary criticism. Once more I express my appreciation to my wife, Muriel Jackson Mellown, for her help and encouragement.

Permissions to quote have been granted by the following: "The Little General" and other quotations from Edwin Muir, *Collected Poems*—Reprinted by permission of Faber and Faber Ltd. from *Collected Poems*, and Oxford University Press (New York); Edwin Muir, *The Estate of Poetry* (1962) and *Essays on Society and Literature* (1949, 1965)—Mr. Gavin Muir and The Hogarth Press, and Harvard University Press; Edwin Muir, *An Autobiography*, *Transition, The Structure of the Novel, Selected Letters of Edwin Muir*, edited by Peter Butter—Mr. Gavin Muir and The Hogarth Press; Willa Muir, *Belonging*—Mr. Gavin Muir and The Hogarth Press; Leonard Woolf, *Downhill All the Way*—The Literary Estate of Leonard Woolf and The Hogarth Press, and Harcourt Brace Jovanovich, Inc.; Virgina Woolf, *A Writer's Diary*—The Literary Estate of Virginia Woolf and The Hogarth Press, and Harcourt Brace Jovanovich, Inc. The frontispiece photograph is reproduced by permission of Mark Gerson FIIP.

Chronology

1887   Edwin Muir born May 15 on island of Pomona in the Orkney Islands, the youngest son of James and Elizabeth (Cormack) Muir.

1901   The Muirs move to Glasgow, where the older sons are employed. From 1901 to 1912 Edwin works in various Glasgow offices as a junior clerk.

1902   Edwin's parents and two older brothers, Willie and Johnnie, die in the next five years.

1912   Edwin works in the office of a bone-rending factory in Greenock and contributes poems to the *New Age* under the pseudonym "Edward Moore."

1914   Begins work as a costing clerk in a Glasgow shipyard, meanwhile writing notes and epigrams for the *New Age*.

1918   *We Moderns* published. In September meets Willa Anderson.

1919   On June 7 Willa and Edwin are married and move to London. He works as an assistant editor for the *New Age*, as dramatic correspondent for the *Scotsman*, as a book reviewer for the *Athenaeum* and other journals, and begins a course of analysis with Dr. Maurice Nicoll.

1920   *We Moderns* published in America with an introduction by H. L. Mencken.

1921   Van Wyck Brooks asks Muir to contribute to the *Freeman*. The Muirs leave London, going to Prague (1921 - 1922) and Dresden (1922 - 1923), and then to Forte dei Marmi, Italy, to Salzburg, and Vienna. They begin their translations from the German.

1924   *Latitudes* published. The Muirs return to England.

1925   *First Poems* published.

1926   The Muirs move to St. Tropez and then Mentone. *Chorus of the Newly Dead* and *Transition* published.

1927   The Muirs move to Dormansland, Surrey; their only child, Gavin, is born in October. *The Marionette* published.

1928 The Muirs move to Crowborough; *The Structure of the Novel* published.

1929 *John Knox, Portrait of a Calvinist* published.

1930 The Muirs translate Franz Kafka's *The Castle*.

1931 *The Three Brothers* published.

1932 The Muirs move to Hampstead; they translate Hermann Broch's *The Sleepwalkers. Six Poems* and *Poor Tom* published.

1934 *Variations on a Time Theme* published.

1935 The Muirs move to St. Andrews, Scotland. *Scottish Journey* and *Social Credit and the Labour Party* published.

1936 *Scott and Scotland* published.

1937 *Journeys and Places* published.

1939 Willa severely ill. *The Present Age* published.

1940 Edwin takes a clerical job; Willa returns to teaching. *The Story and the Fable* published.

1941 Willa and Edwin severely ill.

1942 Muir appointed to the British Council Staff in Edinburgh; is in charge of various International Houses.

1943 *The Narrow Place* published.

1945 Muir appointed Director of the British Institute in Prague; lectures on English literature at the Charles University.

1946 Muir delivers the W. P. Ker Memorial lecture in Glasgow. *The Voyage* and *The Scots and Their Country* published.

1947 Charles University and the University of Edinburgh award Muir honorary doctorates; other honorary degrees follow in later years.

1948 The Muirs leave Prague; Edwin suffers a nervous breakdown.

1949 Edwin named Director of the Rome Institute of the British Council. *Essays on Literature and Society* and *The Labyrinth* published.

1950 Rome Institute closed; Edwin becomes Warden of Newbattle Abbey College, Dalkeith.

1952 *Collected Poems, 1921 - 1951*, edited by John C. Hall, published.

1953 On the Coronation List of Honours, Edwin named Companion of the British Empire; also elected Fellow of the Royal Society of Literature.

1954 *An Autobiography* published.

1955 At Harvard as the Charles Eliot Norton Professor of Poetry for 1955 - 1956.

Chronology

1956   The Muirs purchase their first house, Priory Cottage, in Swaffham Prior, Cambridgeshire. *One Foot in Eden* published.

1959   On January 3 Edwin Muir dies in a Cambridge nursing home.

1960   *Collected Poems, 1921 - 1958*, edited by Willa Muir and John C. Hall, published.

1962   *The Estate of Poetry* (the Norton lectures), with foreword by Archibald MacLeish, published.

1965   *Essays on Literature and Society* (enlarged edition) and *Selected Poems*, with preface by T. S. Eliot, published.

1974   *Selected Letters of Edwin Muir*, edited and introduced by P. H. Butter, published.

CHAPTER 1

Biography

E DWIN Muir stands apart from other major twentieth-century
poets because he uses poetry to express a traditional philosophy
based on a religious understanding of life. While he frequently attains
in his poems an aesthetic level that requires no apologies, it is his attitude to life that places his work in the tradition of Wordsworth,
Vaughan, and Traherne and makes it prized by so many readers. This
attitude was directly shaped by Muir's personal experiences, and thus
one most appropriately comes to Edwin Muir's writings by looking
first at the writer's life.[1]

I Early Influences: The Orkney Background

The most important shaping force on Muir's literary production
was his birth and upbringing in the Orkney Islands, to the north of the
mainland of Scotland. His father was a tenant farmer, and he was the
youngest child of his elderly parents. In this remote, northernmost
part of the British Isles, the farmers and fishermen knew a timeless
way of life that derived from traditions existing long before the Industrial Revolution. It was essentially an agrarian life which was
aware of time only as the passing of the seasons and which was in contact with an archetypal order of life. The stability of this world came
from its psychological wholeness, for there was a meaning and a
center to the private and communal lives of individuals. After Muir
had grown up and left the Orkneys, he looked back to this life and
recognized it as an almost mythical, ideal way for man to live. Thus in
dealing with the chaos of twentieth-century life, he was able to
describe another sort of life and, unlike other poets, to put forward not
merely an ideal, but an actual alternative. This awareness of a good
way of life gives Muir's poems and philosophical writings a concrete,
affirmative quality which sets them apart from those of his contemporaries.

Hardly less influential was the young Edwin's religious orientation to life. The Muir family attended the United Presbyterian Church and, like their neighbors, were caught up in the great religious revivals which swept across the British Isles in the late nineteenth century. Though the daily lives of the Orkney farmers were patterned by timeless nature, their religious attitudes were dictated by strict Calvinism. They knew Hell and Salvation from it for the Elect as real entities, and they accepted without question the authority of the Bible, which they interpreted literally. They emphasized such Old Testament concepts as restrictions and punishments, rather than the New Testament ideas of an Incarnate Deity and the need for love and mercy. *An Autobiography* shows that Edwin, a highly sensitive, introverted child, fell prey to a sense of guilt and fear that tormented him in various ways during his childhood and that intensified the sexual problems of adolescence. He experienced several religious "conversions" before he turned away in his young manhood from formal religion; and it was not until he reached late middle age that he again showed an interest in religion as such, and indeed he never returned to formal religious practices.

Although Edwin Muir was to become a recognized authority on some of the most difficult writing of the twentieth century, his schooling began and ended in the Orkneys. Being a sickly child and needed on the farm as well, he spent the minimum amount of time in the rural Orkney schools, enjoying a full year of uninterrupted lessons only when the family moved into the town of Kirkwall. The next year, when Edwin was fourteen, the Muirs moved to Glasgow and he left school for good. The largest part of his education actually came from his later years of wide reading.

II   *Life in Glasgow*

The young boy's idyllic life in the Orkneys came into even sharper contrast when Edwin was taken to Glasgow in 1901. It was one of the most industrialized cities in Europe, exemplifying the worst qualities of the modern way of life. The farm family from the Orkneys could not adjust to the city life and within a few years Edwin's mother, father, and two brothers were dead, and Edwin was left on his own. Because he could see only anarchy and confusion in Glasgow, Muir remembered the Orkneys as a place of order and meaning, forgetting the religious difficulties he had known there. The contrast which he felt at this time to exist between the two places stands behind almost everything he was ever to write, while the sense of loss and of aimlessness which he experienced in these crucial years of development continued to plague him even in his old age.

The story of the young Edwin Muir in Glasgow in the prewar and war years is that of a talented youth laboring under severe emotional and physical handicaps, educating himself in literature and languages, and trying to express his ideas. Muir was helped in his struggle to overcome the disadvantages of his birth and environment by A. R. Orage, editor of the *New Age*.[2] Muir had become a regular reader of this weekly newspaper in 1909 or 1910. It was then probably the most advanced journal published in England, presenting a clear, unbiased report of contemporary cultural activities. Because of his admiration for its writers and his respect for its policies, Muir asked Orage for advice in overcoming his intellectual problems. Orage told him to study a writer until he felt that he knew how a great mind operated. Muir began reading Nietzsche, who immediately gave him a philosophy which stood in place of his discarded religion and which never completely left him, even in his last years. Orage also printed various notes, poems, and epigrams which Muir sent to him, including one series of short, aphoristic notes in imitation of Nietzsche that was published during 1916 - 1917 under the title "We Moderns." In 1918 Orage persuaded his friend Stanley (later Sir Stanley) Unwin of Allen and Unwin Publishers to issue the notes as a volume with the same title, some of the epigrams being included as an appendix. Although in later years Muir almost disowned the book because he felt that it belied his mature character, the genesis of his intellectual development can be found in it. This beginning point is Nietzsche, whom Muir quotes and appeals to as an authority, and whose presence is felt on every page. Edwin Muir ended his career as a traditional, Christian Platonist, but he began as an avant-garde, iconoclastic Nietzschean.

III *Marriage*

The last of these major influences upon Muir's literary work is his marriage. In 1918 Edwin was introduced to Willa Anderson, a native of the Shetland Islands who had been brought up in Montrose; she had graduated M.A. at St. Andrews University with first-class honors in classics and had begun a teaching career. Willa and Edwin were married in a London Registry Office on 7 June 1919. Their marriage was all important to Edwin's literary aspirations, for, as a *Times* writer later remarked, his wife's "more emphatic personality, and also perhaps quicker practical sense, contributed profoundly to his life and in a large measure made it possible for him to do what he did."³ Willa Muir provided the resolution of purpose and the determination he lacked, becoming the authority figure whom he had always needed. Muir was gratefully aware of her influence: "If my wife had not encouraged me," he writes in *An Autobiography,* "it is unlikely that I should have taken the plunge myself [to become a professional writer]; I was still paralysed by my inward conflict. My marriage was the most fortunate event in my life."⁴

IV   *Early Recognition of Muir as a Psychological Critic*

In 1919 the young married couple moved to London; and within a few months Edwin secured enough writing assignments to support them. In the next two years he established himself in the London literary world, proving his worth through a steady production of reviews, notes, and essays, and making such contacts with editors and publishers that he rarely had difficulty in later years in placing his work. At the same time he began a course of Jungian analysis with Dr. Maurice Nicoll.⁵ While it was never completed, and even though the Muirs discounted its influence, obviously Dr. Nicoll hastened and facilitated Muir's personal development, as well as teaching him enough Freudian and Jungian theory to make him one of the foremost psychological critics of literature in the 1920s. Muir's prowess as a psychological critic can be seen in the essay "A Plea for Psychology in Literary Criticism," which he published in January 1921.⁶ One of his main points at this time is the demand that the critic look at the work, and not at the writer, an attitude that aligned him with the academic developments in criticism which were to come from Cambridge and, in America, from John Crowe Ransom and his friends at Vanderbilt and Kenyon. This essay (like his other critical writings of this period) also reveals his willingness, even eagerness, to promote new writers and new ways of criticism, qualities that were to help make him one of the most respected critics of contemporary literature in the next several decades. The essay also marks Muir's success in London, for it was published alongside essays by some of the most noted writers of the day, including those by T. S. Eliot which were later collected in *The Sacred Wood.*

While Muir was working in London, his first book, *We Moderns,* was gaining him an American public. In 1919 the New York publisher

Alfred A. Knopf was publishing new philosophical works in a series entitled the "Free Lance Books," each being introduced by H. L. Mencken. Knopf published *We Moderns* as the fourth book in the series in 1920. In the introduction Mencken writes mainly about Nietzsche and his influence on contemporary America, but he declares that "Mr. Muir not only has Nietzsche behind him; he also has Freud," thus placing the incontrovertible mark of modernity upon Muir.[7] This publication brought Muir's name before American editors and publishers, who remembered him as a provocative critic of contemporary life and literature and who later bought and published his writings.

V   *The Move to the Continent and Later Life*

By 1921, then, Edwin Muir had established himself as a promising young critic; but it was the experiences of the next three years that helped him become a poet. In the summer he was given contracts and assurances that the New York *Freeman* and the London *New Age* would publish any essays and reviews that he sent to them, and with this dollar and sterling income he and Willa joined the crowd of Anglo-American expatriates living on the Continent. Freed from the routine of daily office schedules and with leisure hours for the first time since his childhood, he read and studied English and European literature and began to write poems. In these years on the Continent he began to understand himself and his life, and the peculiar psychological strength and veracity in his writings originates in this period.

There were other changes, for the Muirs realized that their allegiance was due not so much to Scotland—and even less to England—as to Europe, and that theirs was the European cultural heritage. This realization had two practical effects. It tended to push Edwin Muir further away from contemporary Scottish writers, many of whom were caught up in the Scottish Nationalist movement, and toward European writers and movements. It also helped to turn him toward translating as a profession and toward his role as the introducer of European writers to the Anglo-American public.

During the 1920s and 1930s Edwin Muir's reviews, essays, and translations (the latter in collaboration with his wife, Willa) made him known to the larger reading public as one of the most respected of the professional literary critics. To a smaller audience he was known as a poet, although even his admirers conceded that his poems were characterized by an overly "literary" flavor and were often derivative in tone.

Then, in 1939, Edwin underwent a religious experience that gave him a new insight into the meaning of his life and of his art; and gradually, after 1939, his poems began to express his newly realized philosophy and to attain an artistic wholeness that had hitherto been absent. The Muirs had returned to Scotland in 1935 to settle in St. Andrews; but they were not happy in this academic community, and Willa's health was rapidly deteriorating. With the outbreak of war, the market for German translations ended; newspapers went on to a strict rationing of paper and cut out all nonessential literary items; and the Muirs had no income.

In this bleak period of poverty, emotional depression, and ill health, Edwin was overcome by a feeling of positive religious commitment. While undressing for bed one night when Willa was in the hospital, he realized, he later wrote, that he was a Christian. He had found himself saying the Lord's Prayer, and "while I went on I grew more composed; as if it had been empty and craving and were being replenished, my soul grew still; every word had a strange fullness of meaning which astonished and delighted me."[8] This experience led him to the realization that "quite without knowing it, I was a Christian, no matter how bad a one. . . . I read the New Testament many times during the following months, particularly the Gospels. I did not turn to any church, and my talks with ministers and divines cast me back upon the Gospels again, which was probably the best thing that could have happened."[9] If Muir's statement of his Christian convictions is accepted at face value (and there is no reason not to do so), and if one remembers that he did not because of this realization forget or put by him the thoughts and experiences of his previous years, then one gains an appropriate critical basis from which to study his post-1940 poems. That many of his critics have been unwilling so to read his poems has been due both to their personal beliefs and to the fact that Willa never shared her husband's religious faith and discouraged further direct statements of it. As Muir wrote, he did not become a churchgoing, witnessing Christian, except insofar as his poems can be accepted as statements of his faith. Since the Nietzschean questioning and psychological doubts which had plagued him in the past did not dissolve in the face of this rediscovered faith, and since his poetic expression was now more or less formed in terms of such an outlook, one must hold this religious experience in mind if one wishes to find the complete meaning of a particular poem, for the poem itself may not provide the means by which it is to be read.

In the midst of their physical troubles, then, spiritual reassurance came to Edwin (Willa, to her last days, could not bring herself to believe in an afterlife and held tenaciously to the "advanced" ideas of her youth); but their worldly problems did not end. In these first dark years of the war Willa went back to teaching, but Edwin, with no official qualifications, could only find work as a clerical helper in a food-stamp office. The end of this unhappy period came in 1942 when Edwin received an appointment to the British Council staff in Edinburgh, where he supervised various International Houses set up by the Council for the use of the foreign nationals who were working with the Allies in Scotland. The work kept him constantly busy and always meeting new people; and almost immediately his gloom and unhappiness lifted and he began to write poems with ever-increasing frequency. These poems herald his appearance as a mature poet, and this Edinburgh period in general marks the beginning of the final, triumphant phase of his literary and professional career.

VI *The Postwar Years*

After the war Edwin continued his association with the British Council, first as director of the British Institute in Prague, where he served from 1945 to 1948, and then as director of the Institute in Rome from 1949 to 1950. The Muirs' stay in Prague during the politically troubled years just after the war (they finally left because of the oppressive quality of life under the Communist regime) brought home to Edwin the predicament of man in the modern world and encouraged him to express man's contemporary situation in his poems. In Italy, however, his understanding of Christianity was broadened. Everywhere he saw representations of the Holy Family. Nothing in his previous religious experiences in the Orkney Presbyterian churches, he wrote in *An Autobiography*, told him "by any outward sign that the Word had been made flesh," but in Italy the representations of that Christ who "was born in the flesh and had lived on earth . . . [were] to be seen everywhere, not only in churches, but on the walls of houses, at cross-roads in the suburbs, in wayside shrines in the parks, and in private rooms. . . . That these images should appear everywhere, reminding everyone of the Incarnation, seemed to me natural and right. . . ."[10] This religious-aesthetic experience is a significant influence upon the poems which Muir wrote in the last decade of his life.

In these years Muir made a name for himself as a teacher and lecturer, and when the British Council closed the Rome Institute, he and

Willa returned to Scotland, where he became the warden of Scotland's only adult-education college, Newbattle Abbey. He enjoyed working with his adult students and was influential in turning several toward literary careers. But he and the directors of the college disagreed over the long-term goals of the institution, and in 1955 he resigned his post.

He left with considerable aplomb, for he had been appointed the Charles Eliot Norton Professor at Harvard for 1955 - 1956. He and Willa were in the United States for the academic year so that he could give the required six lectures; they were subsequently published as *The Estate of Poetry*. Returning to England, the Muirs were able to buy a house in Swaffham Prior, Cambridgeshire, and here Edwin Muir wrote his last poems, while still supporting himself by writing book reviews. Under the sponsorship of the Bollingen Foundation he began writing a book on the Scottish ballads (it was unfinished at his death, and Willa took over the grant, publishing her book *Living with Ballads* in 1965). After a period of gradually deteriorating health at the end of 1958, he died in Cambridge on 3 January 1959. His body was buried in the parish churchyard at Swaffham Prior. Willa continued to live in their home until the illnesses of age forced her to leave the rather isolated village. She occupied a flat in Kathleen Raine's London home until her condition demanded that she enter a nursing home. Willa Muir died on 22 May 1970; she was buried next to Edwin in Swaffham Prior.

CHAPTER 2

The Professional Journalist

I N his lifetime Edwin Muir was perhaps best known to the British reading public as a critic of contemporary fiction, although editors and publishers considered him an all-round professional writer who could be counted on for interesting essays and books on almost any topic. He and his wife, Willa Muir, were acknowledged to be among the best translators of contemporary German novels. The largest part of his writings is composed of miscellaneous reviews, commissioned books, and translations. Critics of Edwin Muir's poems have often passed over these various prose writings, yet they are important in themselves and they frequently reveal some of the background to and influences upon Muir's imaginative work.

I Book Reviews

In 1919 Willa and Edwin moved to London, and in a short time he was contributing to a number of newspapers, while working as a part-time assistant on the weekly *New Age*, the journal he had read so carefully during his Glasgow years. The larger part of this apprentice work consisted of writing book reviews for the *New Age* and the *Athenaeum*, the weekly newspaper which John Middleton Murry was currently editing. These early reviews show Muir developing the skills in which he was later to excel. The best quality of these critical writings is their directness and their general lack of bias. In attempting to estimate the value of contemporary poets (who he knew would actually read his reviews) Muir moved away from the negative attitude that characterized his first book, *We Moderns*, and toward his future position as a promoter of new writers. In only a relatively short time he wrote his reviews with increasingly greater assurance; and as the years passed, his positive, encouraging attitude toward new writers and his serious approach to reviewing never faltered. Although obviously time has robbed many of his initial reactions of their value, his conscientious approach makes a surprisingly large amount of this literary journalism still worth reading. Leonard Woolf, one of the most levelheaded of men, looked back in his autobiography *Downhill All the Way* (1967) at some of the literary men whom he had known, particularly during his tenure as literary editor of the *Nation*, and declared that Muir was "an admirable critic" who "was so sensitive, intelligent, and honest minded that, as a serious critic, he always had something of his own worth saying even about masterpieces buried long ago under mountains and monuments of criticism. But even in the ephemeral and debased form of criticism, reviewing, he was remarkable. For a long time [August 1924 to May 1928, to be exact] he used to review novels for me in the *Nation*, a mechanized, mind-destroying occupation for most people. For him it never became mechanical and his mind's eye was as clear and lively after a year of it as when he began."[1]

The eighty-odd reviews Muir wrote for the *Nation* contain much valuable literary criticism. Looking at D. H. Lawrence's novels Muir is confused by the "patchy" qualities of *St. Mawr* and *The Princess* and writes that Lawrence's "inspiration fails again and again, but he flings the second-rate and the palpably histrionic at his reader with the same conviction as he shows when he is at his best."[2] Later he declares that *The Plumed Serpent* is "an outpouring of anything and everything; it does not so much lose, as defeat, its effect."[3] Muir dislikes Lawrence's using fiction to express philosophy, not because of the damage done to the form of the novel, but because fiction makes it more difficult to comprehend Lawrence's philosophy. Another review is of three of the Hogarth Essays: Mrs. Woolf's *Mr. Bennett and Mrs. Brown;* Roger Fry's *The Artist and Psycho-Analysis;* and T. S. Eliot's *Homage to Dryden.* Not unexpectedly Muir praises all three studies, although he feels that Fry's "has come too soon; the students of psycho-analysis have said nothing illuminating upon art yet." Eliot's enigmatic criticism puzzles the more outspoken Muir, yet he appreciates both Eliot and Mrs. Woolf.[4] Muir's reviews of books requiring specialized knowledge—biographies and studies of such authors as Melville, de Maupassant, and Swinburne—are especially interesting as evidence of the way in which he overcame his limited knowledge by a close reading of the books before him and by applying his common sense to them.[5] These reviews also show his reaction to popular taste: he champions writers like Swinburne who were currently neglected by critics; and he attacks those like Henry James who were the favorites of the literary cognoscenti.[6] These reviews are a record of Muir's public education, for the specific knowledge he uses in later literary studies can often be traced back to the books he reviewed.

In the late 1920s Edwin and Willa found themselves so occupied with translating and with their own imaginative writing that Edwin gave up regular book-reviewing, and it was not until 1932 that he began writing reviews again, his first contributions being to the *Spectator*. Then, in January 1933, he took over the fortnightly review of fiction for the *Listener* which Eric Linklater had previously written. In the next twelve years—to September 1945—he wrote some three hundred reviews for the *Listener*, each review averaging about two thousand words in length. He generally considered three novels or collections of short stories, mentioning other novels as "recommended." These reviews thus provide a record of the initial reaction of a sensitive critic to practically all of the important works of fiction published in these years, and—since the estimate of these novelists is generally that which prevails today—evidence that Muir may have helped to shape current attitudes toward Ivy Compton-Burnett, Graham Greene, Evelyn Waugh, and other such novelists.

Between 1933 and 1944 Muir reviewed six novels by Ivy Compton-Burnett, declaring of *More Women than Men* that "Dialogue . . . should be a form of art, something more than a mere indication that the characters have the use of their tongues."[7] He always notices a novelist's attitude to life, and his demand that a writer evince a meaningful understanding lies behind much of his criticism. But since the *Listener* series includes only fiction, he is forced to recognize the technical problems of the novelist. He gives particular attention to the creation of believable characters, accepting a stylized presentation if it results in true-to-life figures, but always wanting three-dimensional characters. This demand, reasonable as it may appear, prevents his appreciating Graham Greene, whom he consistently criticizes for cavalier treatment of characters. In *A Gun for Sale* (American title, *This Gun for Hire*) Greene draws "vivid" characters, but the vividness is so great that the characters "sometimes look like caricatures."[8] Ida and Pinkie in *Brighton Rock* do not convince Muir, although the novel itself is "a sincere comment on our life which deserves serious attention."[9] *The Confidential Agent* at last gives Muir an understanding of Greene: his "stories are the description of a hunt. The hunter's quarry is the individual; the hunter is society, a steel monster, heartless and glittering, oiled and set going by people who live in houses which are too rich and comfortable. Generally the

fugitive has no chance, for the machine that pursues him also pro
duced him, and is both the original offender and the hangman.
Consequently there is nothing but a close [sic] circle, filled with anger
and injustice and faint, unavailing pity, as in *Brighton Rock*. . . ."[10]
This partly accurate but incomplete criticism is similar to the evaluation of Evelyn Waugh. In *A Handful of Dust* Waugh "denies to his
characters any moral sense at all, and that makes them untrue, and
their story meaningless."[11] The characters in *Work Suspended* are
like puppets, and Waugh is "a conjuror who explains the secret of a
trick while he is performing it."[12] Muir rarely appreciates satire; and
he generally turns away from criticism which is other than direct and
open.

Muir also reviews the writers whom he wrote about earlier in avant-
garde periodicals (I will discuss these essays in the next chapter); and,
although he is writing in the *Listener* for the general public, he
neither makes concessions to popular taste nor writes down to his
audience. The only difference between his reviews of Aldous Huxley,
D. H. Lawrence, and James Joyce and his consideration of them in
earlier studies is that the *Listener* allowed him less space for
thoroughly argued criticism. In his *Transition* essay (1926) he
criticizes Huxley for his lack of imagination; while reading *Eyeless in
Gaza* he can see a change in the novelist:[13]

Mr. Huxley has always had an unusually clear and direct perception of the
humiliating treacheries of the appetites; his imagination is always at its best
when he deals with them. He deals with them in this book too, but he has
something to set against them, and the result is that his treatment of them is
far more pointed than it ever has been before. What he sets against them is a
recognition of the need for moral effort, and a recognition that moral effort is
possible. That really amounts to a change in the focus of his imagination, and
one of the most interesting results is that it has greatly intensified his imagination and made it more generally valid. The characters in his other books are
somewhat fabulous, whereas in this story they give us the undeniable feeling
of being human beings.[14]

In reviewing the posthumously published *Tales of D. H. Lawrence*,
Muir synthesizes his earlier ideas, remarking that "it has become a
literary canon that Lawrence is at his best in his short stories. Yet," he
continues in his typical, common-sense manner, "if he had written
nothing but them we should have a very inadequate idea of his
powers."

His long novels, it is true, are full of outrageous faults; his vision of life as he sees it almost always becomes confused at a certain point with his vision of life as he would like it to be; his characters turn into symbols; he remodels them quite arbitrarily without waiting for experience to do it for him; it is as if he were suddenly impatient with life and could no longer endure the drudgery of describing it, seeing that it might have been so different and so much more beautiful. So, except, perhaps, for *The Rainbow*, every one of his novels, while rich in separate beauties, misses beauty as a whole, for before it can achieve that, an adventitious beauty, frailer than that which would have been won by accepting life as it is to the end, is impatiently superimposed. Yet only the long novel could have given him scope for the flow of his genius, or for the "flow" that he mentioned so often and that seemed so necessary to him; and if at one point or another it seemed fated to deviate from reality and lose itself among chaotic symbols, the reader had at least the pleasure of watching the splendid spectacle while it lasted. His short stories represent at most a short spurt of that impetuous energy.[15]

Through the 1930s Muir reviewed the individual sections of James Joyce's *Finnegans Wake* (the "Work in Progress," as it was called) as they were published in various periodicals and, questioning always the possible effect that contemporary writing might have upon literary tradition, came to mainly negative conclusions about Joyce's work. When *Finnegans Wake* was published as a whole in 1939, Muir devoted an entire *Listener* review to it, although he admitted that he could not hope to understand the work after only a fortnight's study. Indeed he found it to be incomprehensible, and he could not get over his suspicion that the novel might be a gigantic leg-pull. "For long stretches," he writes, "the book reads like a long private joke, the elaborate blarney of an insatiable linguist."[16] Although he was puzzled by *Finnegans Wake*, he remained true to his task of promoting new, difficult writing and dutifully informed his readers of Joyce's latest developments. This review also allowed him clearly to express his standard that the effective use of language determines the value of a novel, or, at least, provides the most absolute standard of judgment.

To read through these reviews confirms Mrs. Leavis's statement that "even when reviewing fiction for the B.B.C. [Muir was] notable for his integrity and his grasp of standards."[17] For twelve years Muir considered the weekly crop of novels without ever aligning himself with any particular faction, or allowing his personal feelings to influence his aesthetic judgment. He experienced personal hardships during this period; he suffered—like his readers—from wartime privations; yet his critical estimates remain detached and unaffected by his own temporal situation. Loyal to a standard of artistic excellence and concerned always that writers provide a serious treatment of life, Edwin Muir conscientiously attempted to write valid criticism of contemporary fiction for his reading public. The respect in which his opinions were held by that public can be deduced from the frequent appearance of quotations from his *Listener* reviews in publishers' advertisements and on the dust jackets of new books.

The novelists about whom Muir wrote studied his comments, reveling in his praise and despairing in his condemnation. Mrs. Woolf's spirits fail when Muir confirms her own opinion of *The Years*; and she quotes his *Listener* review in her diary: "E.M. says *The Years* is dead and disappointing. . . . All the lights sank; my reed bent to the ground. Dead and disappointing—so I'm found out and that odious rice pudding of a book is what I thought it—a dank failure."[18] J. B. Priestley, writing in his autobiography, points to *Daylight on Saturday* (1943) as one of his most important books and remarks with pride that "Edwin Muir, not an easy man to please is quoted [on the jacket of the book] as saying, in a *Listener* review, that this was by far my best novel."[19] And George Barker gratefully remembers in his essay "Coming to London" that Muir reviewed his first novel, *Alanna Autumnal* (1933), in the *Listener* and later asked him to call.[20] For both readers and writers Muir's *Listener* reviews were of great value.

Muir also wrote two or three reviews each month between January 1935, and November 1939 for the *Scotsman*, considering one nonfictional work in each review. He and James Milne, the popular essayist, were the only reviewers to have a byline; and his reviews were always printed in the same place, the upper left-hand corner of the book-review page. He reviewed mainly literary studies, although he also wrote about translations of the poetry of Baudelaire, Rilke, Mallarmé, and other Continental poets.[21] These pieces are more like short essays than reviews, for obviously such studies as Edward Sackville-West's biography of De Quincey, *Flame in Sunlight* and E. M. Forster's *Abinger Harvest* gave Muir far more to write about than did many contemporary novels.[22] He praises T. S. Eliot's *Family Reunion*, and he writes enthusiastically about F. R. Leavis's *Revaluations* and reproves R. D. Jameson for using I. A. Richards's vocabulary in *Comparisons of Literature* "without [Richards's] other attributes."[23] Muir later repeated many of these critical judgments in his literary study *The Present Age* (1939).

The last of these series of reviews began in 1949 for the London *Observer*, for which Muir wrote one or two reviews every month until his death. These pieces take the form of essays occasioned by the book in question. Muir's critical approach was always essentially subjective, and since he was here drawing upon thirty or more years of experience, these *Observer* reviews reveal both his mature critical powers and some of his standards. He generally disliked academic critics who approached literature from a rigidly doctrinal point of view that fails to appreciate the human spirit embodied in a work of art. As Muir grew older he relaxed his own earlier standards, for while he had once praised the ideals of the "new critics," now in the 1950s he consistently used Cleanth Brooks as a whipping boy for analytical criticism.[24] One review in particular contains a full statement of Muir's critical tenets in his last years; it is of Harold Osborne's *Aesthetics and Criticism.* Muir points out that Osborne sets up five "main aesthetic assumptions which are embodied in modern criticism" and then holds that unless a critic "describes or arranges works of art in accordance with any one of these five criteria, or any combination of them," he is not writing what may properly be called criticism. Such orthodoxy is the antithesis of Muir's practice; and he expresses his feeling that a critic reaches a judgment through

a long experience of books, poems, writings of all kinds, by which he has learned to distinguish their qualities and assess them, just as in the course of living we learn to distinguish and assess the qualities of people we meet. This method or discipline was the one recommended by Plato for the understanding of objects of beauty. The student was advised to contemplate beautiful objects in an ascending scale of excellence until he became worthy at last to perceive Beauty itself in its ideal perfection. After a long acquaintance with masterpieces I do not think it inconceivable that a rare critic may, without knowing it, come to judge works of art, if not by Plato's standard, at least by the standard which Mr. Osborne sets up in this book. On the other hand he may not, and yet may say something about a writer whom he intimately understands which is worth saying. . . . But he will not say anything of use if his judgment has not been matured by experience.[25]

Rational thought alone is to Muir restricting and conclusive; and total apprehension (which may include nonrational factors) is a better guide. For all his aesthetic principles, Muir believed that literature is never more than man himself, and he refused to set up absolute standards for works of art. Each must be judged on its own particular merits, although the critic must see it in the light of the artist's general philosophy of life.

This constant reviewing had certain beneficial effects, for while

financial necessity kept Muir on the reviewer's treadmill, the reading
which it forced upon him provided information for his original essays;
and the act of criticism made him develop his own ideas. Yet the true
significance of this and the other journalism actually lies in its influence upon Muir's poems. The drift of his first poems quite clearly
shows that he could easily have turned his back upon the world of activity; and had he not been forced to support himself through such
journalism, his later poems would not have embodied that understanding of the real world which is one of their best qualities.

II *Commissioned Books*

Although practically all of Muir's nonfictional prose might be
labeled journalism, I shall consider in a separate chapter those books
dealing primarily with literary matters and notice here only those
works peripheral to his literary interests which he would not have
written had he not been commissioned to do so.

A. John Knox *(1929)*

The first of these miscellaneous studies is the biography which the
publisher Jonathan Cape commissioned, *John Knox, Portrait of a
Calvinist.* Although undertaken as a commercial venture, the
biography allowed Muir to express himself on the subject of Scotland
and Calvinism, and thus opened the way to his better understanding
of himself in relationship to his native land. The research for the book
also taught him about the historical period to which he increasingly
attached so much importance, deciding that the Reformation ended a
"natural" way of life and brought about the "false" life of modern
times. He read Knox's writings and various biographies in an attempt
to understand the man whose influence had lasted so long because he
wanted "to give a critical account of a representative Calvinist and
Puritan. The temper in which I have attempted this," he continues,
"may perhaps best be described as realistic; I assume, for example,
that terms such as predestination and election do not actually describe
for the present age the change which took place in Knox's life, and I
assume equally that his firm conviction of his prophetic powers was a
delusion. . . . I have attempted to tell in contemporary terms how a
typical Calvinist and Puritan lived, felt and thought. . . ."[26] Muir's
intention is in keeping with his role as a psychological critic, but he
falls (as he later admits in *An Autobiography*) into the subjectivism

which amateur psychologists so rarely escape: his "dislike for Knox
and certain things in Scottish life" biased his understanding.[27] Too,
he attempts to apply the principles of psychological behavior to the
written evidence, not allowing for historical differences. Actually this
personal bias distinguishes *John Knox* from many of the other popular
biographies of the period and helps make it an eminently readable
book. For example, when Muir writes of the death of Mary, the Queen
Regent, he gives a damning analysis of Knox's character:

Mary of Guise . . . had remained so securely beyond the reach of [Knox's]
admonitions and furies. She had encountered with irony his claims to
prophetship; she had met his fiercest threats with smiling self-control. Her
virtues were so antipathetic to him that he could only see in them a cloak for
deep-seated vices. He hated her self-possession, her patience, her modera-
tion, for they were virtues which, as he was quite incapable of them, he
neither understood not [sic] trusted. . . . But what must have infuriated
him most was her calm refusal to recognize his claims. Against such a woman
he was powerless. There is a disappointment, therefore, as well as spite in his
persistent blackening of her memory. . . . [Muir quotes Knox's *History of
the Reformation*] . . . Knox's hatred and his hope in the end, if not by direct
admonition, then at least by prayer to God, he had got even with Mary, are
equally to be traced in that very repellent passage. If he could not claim the
credit for having made an impression on her, he was resolved at least to have
the responsibility for her dropsy (*JK*, 212 - 14).

In the appendix, "Knox and Scotland," Muir decides that "what
Knox really did was to rob Scotland of all the benefits of the
Renaissance. Scotland never enjoyed these as England did, and no
doubt the lack of that immense advantage has had a permanent
effect. It can be felt, I imagine, even at the present day" (*JK*, 309).
This attitude to the Reformation becomes increasingly important in
Muir's thinking about Scotland's literature and language, and the
biography and this appendix in particular show how these commissioned books shaped Muir's ideas. *John Knox* is analytical
biography and not, like the biographies being written by such contemporaries of Muir as André Maurois and Emil Ludwig, a picturesque recreation of characters and places. Yet Muir's work was not
completely out of step with current writing in the genre, for the popular audience in the 1920s was eager to be told the "truth" about
formerly revered figures; and many writers assumed the stance of the
debunker. Thus while Muir's attitude to Knox rose out of personal
convictions, it was also appropriate for a commercial book. Lytton

Strachey probably did as much as any writer to make such biographies popular, and *John Knox* can certainly be considered one of the many offspring of *Eminent Victorians.*

B.   Scottish Journey *(1935)*
   In the mid-1930s the publishing houses of Heinemann and Gollancz issued a series of "social reports" which were intended to provide an account of life during the economic depression. Sir Phillip Gibbs wrote on Europe (*European Journey,* 1934), and J. B. Priestley, on England (*English Journey,* 1934). Muir's contribution was *Scottish Journey.* His "research" for this book consisted in driving across Scotland in the summer of 1934; and his personal experiences with the antiquated car which he had borrowed for the trip provide a lighthearted relief, as well as a sense of continuity, to the social report.
   Muir describes the land he knew best—Glasgow, Edinburgh, and the Orkneys; and although he puts forward ideas about economics and sociological problems and discusses far-reaching historical concepts, he remains basically a literary man. Driving south from Edinburgh, he ponders over the character of the border people and decides that their "most essential expression" is to be found in the ballads, "the greatest body of Catholic poetry in Scottish literature, greater even than that of Henryson and Dunbar."[28] The border ballads are expressions of the native temperament, just as to the west the love poetry reflects the natural fertility of the land: "The love songs of Dumfriesshire and the Mearns, another region famed for its fertility in Scotland, are mainly Rabelaisian . . . the prevailing attitude to love is expressed in ballads which cannot be quoted in a modern book of travel, and in certain songs of Burns" (*SJ,* 64).
   Scottish Journey even includes Muir's own poems. "My impressions of Edinburgh," he writes, "or rather of historical Scotland, my feeling of the contrast between its legendary past and its tawdry present, crystallised several months after my visit in a poem." He imagines that he can see and hear "The Miller's daughter walking by / With frozen fingers soldered to her basket," and that the sound of her "light heels" mocks all the dead heroes of Scotland and "all the singers." The dead are "powerless," and the living "are content / With their poor frozen life and shallow banishment" (*SJ,* 38). When Muir writes about Glasgow, he expresses himself twice in Audenesque verse. The first poem (neither was ever reprinted) introduces the chapter on Glasgow and is a satiric ballad on the foibles of Scottish conventions, suggesting that "Scottish cattle . . . sleek

and proud" are better cared for than the Scots themselves (*SJ*, 100 - 101). The second poem "took shape during [his] journey through the industrial regions, and arose from a sense of the violent contrasts." Again Muir places images of the "haves" and "have-nots" side by side, concluding with a static picture:

> At the big house the Owner waits his doom
> While his Rhine-maiden daughters sit and play
>
> Wagner and Strauss. Beneath the railway bridge
> In patient waxwork line the lovers stand.
> Venus weeps overhead. Poised on the ridge
> The unemployed regard the Promised Land
> (*SJ*, 152 - 53).

Although by its nature a dated book, *Scottish Journey* has a personal tone that still appeals to the general reader, while to the social historian it offers a valuable account of the Scottish outlook in a difficult time.

C. Social Credit and the Labour Party (1935), *and other minor works*

The pamphlet *Social Credit and the Labour Party: An Appeal* takes one away from Muir's "commercial" books and toward his more personal writings. After he stopped writing for the *New Age* in 1924, he concentrated on literary subjects; but when Orage founded the *New English Weekly* in 1932 and Muir occasionally contributed to it, he once again considered contemporary social problems. Thus when Stanley Nott, one of Orage's friends and Major Douglas's publisher, brought out a series of "Pamphlets on the New Economics"—that is, the Douglas theory of economics—Muir wrote one of the pamphlets; the other writers included Orage, Ezra Pound, Herbert Read, G. D. H. Cole, and Bonamy Dobrée. Muir's essay is a "letter" addressed to an unidentified person who appears to be a Marxist member of the Labour Party and a Scotsman whom Muir knew in prewar Glasgow days. The gist of Muir's appeal is that while he and his friend believe a social revolution to be both imminent and desirable, they differ on the means by which it should be effected. The Socialist idea of the community's taking over "the means of production, distribution, and exchange" is out of date in 1935, Muir writes.[29] He would reverse the terms of this formula and try to change society by "taking over the means of exchange," utilizing the theories of Social Credit (*SC*, 16).

He stresses that the association of Socialism and Social Credit is his own idea and explains why the two belong together. Although he believes in Social Credit "as the key to the whole practical problem of change, I am convinced that it can do nothing without allying itself with and adopting to a great measure the Marxian point of view and the Marxian technique. As it stands it is a Utopian idea, by which I do not mean that it is not true, but that it has not behind it an historical philosophy, so that it is incapable in itself of producing, as organized Socialism has partly done, an actual historical instrument through which it can be realized" (*SC*, 18).

This carefully structured essay exemplifies the clarity and balance of Muir's prose, as in his pointing out that "the belief of the orthodox Communist seems to be that once the revolution has worked out its task society will begin with a clean sheet, and the effects of the bloodshed and suffering be wiped away. I can only say that such things do not happen, and have never happened in history. . . . It is comparatively easy to destroy institutions and even systems; it is in-finitely difficult to *produce* a civilization out of the resulting débris, no matter how admirable the new institutions or the new system may be" (*SC*, 9, 12). The desired social change must be accomplished peacefully, hopefully through the adoption of Social Credit. The pamphlet is actually a practical application of Muir's ideas about time, which are found also in his poems of the 1930s: society, like the individual, must examine its history to find a guide into the future.

Other books which Muir was commissioned to write include the letterpress to *Poles in Uniform* (1943), an album of sketches of the Polish army in England by the artist Aleksander Żyw.[30] Two years later Muir wrote a pamphlet entitled *The Scots and Their Country* (1945) for the British Council Series, "The British People, How They Live and Work."[31] The little books in this series are examples of postwar propaganda in which the British government attempted to define the British way of life for both friends and former enemies. In spite of this professed aim, Muir's pamphlet is written in the same hypercritical tone of his other writings on Scotland, and he is no less censorious of certain aspects of Scottish life than he is in *John Knox*, in *Scottish Journey*, or in *Scott and Scotland*.

All of these books merit reading, for what *John Knox* may lack in scholarly facts it makes up in readability; and *Scottish Journey* might well be read alongside George Orwell's better-known *The Road to Wigan Pier* (1937) for additional information about Britain in these years. These commissioned books show Edwin Muir's success as a professional writer.

III   *Translations by Edwin and Willa Muir*

In 1920 Alfred Knopf published *We Moderns* with an introduction by H. L. Mencken, who stressed the modernity of the then unknown Muir, emphasizing his knowledge of modern (that is, Freudian) psychology and of Nietzsche. The book was enthusiastically reviewed by Van Wyck Brooks in the *Freeman*, the newly established New York weekly for which Brooks was literary editor. Later in 1920 he and the *Freeman* editors, Francis Neilson (himself an acquaintance of A. R. Orage), Albert Jay Nock, and B. W. Huebsch, accepted and published an essay by Muir. The iconoclastic, Nietzschean-flavored, psychologically oriented attitudes which made Muir's writings acceptable to the *New Age* were precisely those qualities which the *Freeman* wanted from its contributors, and in the summer of 1921 Muir was asked to contribute regularly to the *Freeman*. He was paid sixty dollars for each article, enough to allow the Muirs to leave London and to live on the Continent for the next three years. Here Muir enjoyed the first leisure he had known in his adult life, and during this period he began to write the poems published in *First Poems* (1925). But in 1924 the *Freeman* ceased publication, and he and Willa took refuge with their friend A. S. Neill, who had set up his international school at Rosenau, Austria. While at Rosenau they were asked by B. W. Huebsch, the New York publisher who had been associated with the *Freeman*, to translate one volume of the *Dramatic Works of Gerhardt Hauptmann* (1925). Martin Secker published the book in England (Viking, Huebsch's successor, was the American publisher); and this connection with Secker enabled Muir to urge him to publish Lion Feuchtwanger's novel *Jud Süss*. Secker reluctantly agreed to do so, requiring Feuchtwanger to pay the Muirs for the translating. They were so enthusiastic about the novel that they almost rewrote it; and, certainly due not a little to their efforts, *Jew Süss* (the American title was *Power*) became a best-seller in 1926 and 1927. But since the Muirs had no royalty rights in the translation, they had no share in the financial success of the book; and thus, when Secker gave them Feuchtwanger's *The Ugly Duchess* (1927) to translate, they merely Englished the novel (the stylistic differences between the two novels were remarked upon by several critics).

The success of *Jew Süss* established the Muirs as translators, and for the next fifteen years they were rarely without a translation in hand. I must stress here that I am dealing as much with Willa as with Edwin; for while Willa once wrote to me that when they were working together they "tore a book in two, did half each, then I went over

Edwin's translation and he went over mine, and the result was a
seamless garment,"[32] the facts remain that in the 1920s and 1930s
Edwin produced a large body of original work and that there was
simply not enough time for him to take a very large part in this
translating: his role was largely that of an editor who concentrated on
polishing the style. Thus from 1924 to 1939 Muir was almost constantly reading not only contemporary British writing but also contemporary German novels, and even though the Muir translations—there
are over thirty of them—cannot be examined for evidence of Edwin's
hand, they figure in the background of his imaginative writing, his
work with Kafka and Broch influencing him to an extent not often
realized. This practical concern with European literature constantly
reminded him of the Nietzschean concept of the good European and
helped to make him one of the least provincial of the popular British
critics of his age; it also occasioned several critical essays, as well as the
founding of the *European Quarterly*.

Surveying the Muir translations reveals some of the most important
works of modern literature, some of the best-sellers of the time, and
also some outright trash. The Muirs continued to translate
Feuchtwanger's historical novels, *The Ugly Duchess* being followed
by *Josephus* (1932), *The Jew of Rome* (1935), and *False Nero* (1937;
American title, *Pretender*). They also translated Feuchtwanger's *Two
Anglo-Saxon Plays* (1929) and the novel *Success* (1930), an exposé of
the Nazi party.

The contemporary scene is the setting used by a number of these
novelists. Kurt Heuser, Ernst Lothar, and Heinrich Mann, to name
only three, were typical of the several cynical and world-weary writers
translated by the Muirs, for Germany in the 1930s did not occasion
many happy novels.[33] They translated four of Sholem Asch's accounts
of Polish Jewry, [34] and biographies of Eleanora Duse, Alexander I, and
Cardinal Richelieu, as well as semifictional treatments of Rubens and
of King Christian of Denmark;[35] they also rewrote the translations of
unknown translators; indeed, until the outbreak of war they virtually
ran a translation factory.

In addition to these collaborations, Willa Muir translated six novels
by herself under the pseudonym "Agnes Neill Scott," including four
by Hans Carossa, the Austrian expressionist. *A Roumanian Diary*
(1929), *A Childhood* (1930), *Boyhood and Youth* (1931), and *Doctor
Gion* (1933) are delicate renditions of Carossa's studiedly innocent vision of the world.[36] While Willa was at work translating, Edwin wrote
a sensitive appreciation of Carossa for the American *Bookman*. He

finds in the novels a vision not unlike his own and writes of *Eine Kindheit* and *Verwandlungen einer Jugend:*

There has probably been no books on childhood such as these since mystics like Traherne. By an inflection here and there, by the rhythm of the prose, sweet, tranquil and pure, they do indeed faintly but persistently recall Traherne. But the radiance which lies over them is less bright, and more diffused; it does not come directly from heaven, like Traherne's, but circuitously, through the hidden forces of the earth, which to the child are secretly bound with the heavenly ones. It is imminent in such things as a favorite splinter of granite, or a glass bead which the boy loves to swing against the window-pane; in all animals, in stones and trees, in houses, and especially in the house which is his home. [37]

While obviously Muir was not basically influenced by Carossa, it is very probable that Carossa's novels aided him in defining his attitude to childhood in general and to his own in particular, and hence assisted him in reaching the personal philosophy which he deduced from his childhood experiences.

A. *Hermann Broch and the Muirs*

Willa Muir once remarked to me that, of these many translations, only the novels by Hermann Broch and Franz Kafka were worth her and Edwin's labor; and indeed the Muirs' reputation as translators lives on because they introduced Broch and Kafka to the English-reading public. Kafka has long since achieved an international reputation, but Broch has only slowly become known to the more advanced reading public. In 1931 the Muirs began their translation of *The Sleepwalkers* for Martin Secker, and Muir enthusiastically described the novel to Sydney Schiff as "first rate, and very beautiful, and not unlike Proust in its great truth and psychological subtlety. . . . It is really exciting, really new, and consummate as a work of art."[38] The novel reflects the history of modern Germany; in Muir's words, "the first book is written in one style, the second in another, and the third in a whole medley of styles, the object being to reproduce by these verbal fluctuations a sense of the disintegration of values in Germany in the years leading up to and following the first World War."[39] The translation posed many problems, and in May 1931 Willa Muir requested information from Broch about a certain phrase and praised his accomplishment. Broch replied with copious information about the novel, writing also that his German publisher

had called her the best translator of German (" 'der besten
Übersetzerin aus dem Deutschen' ").[40]
    From this initial correspondence there developed a friendship, and
Edwin wrote an appreciation of Broch for the American *Bookman*
which shows once again the way in which his own ideas were reinforced and strengthened by another writer. "Herr Broch's thesis," he
writes, "is this: that ever since the dissolution of the mediaeval syn-
thesis a disintegration of values has been going on which today has
almost worked itself out."[41] Here is Muir's concept of the "good life"
which existed in the past and is now lost to modern man—for this
translating was occasionally beneficial to Muir, helping him to realize
his position in the larger community of thinkers and to delineate more
clearly the ideas he knew as vague intuitions: Broch's understanding
of history strengthened his own concepts of man's life in the present
age.
    The Sleepwalkers was published in 1932 in England and the United
States, but Broch was too advanced for the time, and over two decades
passed before the novel was given significant critical attention. After
the German invasion of Austria, Broch (who was Jewish by birth) was
detained in prison by the local National Socialists until summer 1938,
when through the efforts of Sydney Schiff, James Joyce, and Muir he
was permitted to leave for England.[42] He lived with the Muirs in St.
Andrews for several months before going on to the United States. His
visit brought Edwin face to face with the social upheavals on the Continent and occasioned the composition of several poems: Broch's
letters from St. Andrews can even be read as glosses to such poems as
"The Refugees."[43] Through all his trials Broch continued to compose
Der Tod des Virgils. He hoped that the Muirs would translate it, but
they did not like the novel. "*The Death of Virgil* was, and remains, a
blind spot to me," Willa declared in 1963, defending herself against
insinuations by Mrs. Jean Starr Untermeyer (the eventual translator
of the novel) that they had refused the work because the pay was inadequate. "I had told Broch," she continued, "impertinently, that
The Death of Virgil was a tombstone on Virgil, with other even more
impertinent remarks which I think Hermann rather enjoyed; at least,
I hope so. Edwin did not like the book any more than I did."[44] In 1940
Willa had been desperately ill and unable to answer Broch's letters;
and the Muirs appear to have had no further contacts with Broch after
1940.

B. *Franz Kafka and the Muirs*

  The introduction of Kafka to English readers was due almost solely to the efforts of the Muirs. They not only translated the major works but also found publishers for them, while Edwin's critical introductions and essays helped to advance Kafka's reputation. The Muirs translated *The Castle* because they believed in Kafka's genius, and, owing to their success with *Jew Süss*, were able to get Martin Secker to publish the novel in 1930. Edwin wrote an "Introductory Note" which, as Wilhelm Emrich observes in his *Franz Kafka* (1958), along with Muir's introductions to *The Great Wall of China* (1933) and *America* (1938), has significantly shaped the public image of Kafka in England and America.[45] Muir interprets the unfamiliar in terms of the familiar, advising that "perhaps the best way to approach *The Castle* is to regard it as a sort of modern *Pilgrim's Progress*, with the reservation, however, that the 'progress' of the pilgrim here will remain in question all the time, and will be itself the chief, the essential problem. *The Castle* is, like *The Pilgrim's Progress*, a religious allegory; the desire of the hero in both cases [is] to work out his salvation. . . ."[46] But since Kafka is "a religious genius" writing in "an age of scepticism," his hero knows only that "the goal and the road indubitably exist, and that the necessity to find them is urgent." The novelist "begins with . . . the barest possible [postulates]; they are roughly these: that there is a right way of life, and that the discovery of it depends on one's attitudes to powers which are almost unknown. What he sets out to do is to find out something about those powers, and the astonishing thing is that he appears to succeed."[47]

  Muir's critical procedure of defining the tradition to which Kafka's work belongs and of criticizing it in terms of that tradition is similar to that used in *Transition*, while the analysis of *The Castle* is related to Muir's own concepts of man's life. Muir's finding one of Kafka's "axioms" to be "that at all times, whatever we may think, the demand of the divine law for unconditional reverence and unconditional obedience is beyond question,"[48] reflects, for example, the conclusion of his dramatic poem "The Field of the Potter" (1932).[49] In it Judas says in reference to Christ, "He chose, and I was chosen. / No one knew Him." Muir's Judas recognizes and bows before the same divine law which the poet finds presented by Kafka. In the *First Poems* (1925) and the *Chorus of the Newly Dead* (1926), written before he read Kafka, Muir frequently considers man's life in terms of the image of the road, while at one point the "Chorus" exclaims: "It was decreed. We cannot tell / Why harlot, idiot or clown / Lived, wept and died. We cannot spell / The hidden word which drove them down." Muir's observation is limited to effects, and he marvels at Kafka's apprehension of causes.

In the 1930s the despair of the period almost caused Muir to doubt man's capacity to understand the "powers" which govern him or even to find his "road." This attitude may be seen in the "Introductory Note" to *The Great Wall of China* (1933). Again Kafka is presented as preeminently a philosopher:

> The problem with which all Kafka's work is concerned is a moral and spiritual one. It is a twofold problem: that of finding one's vocation, one's true place, whatever it may be, in the community; and that of acting in accordance with the will of heavenly powers. But though it has those two aspects it was in his eyes a single problem; for a man's true place in the community is finally determined not by secular, but by divine, law, and only when, by apparent chance or deliberate effort, a man finds himself in his divinely appointed place, can he live as he should. Many people slip into their place without being aware of it; others are painfully conscious of the difficulty, the evident impossibility, of finding any place at all; and nobody has been more clearly and deeply conscious of it, I think, than Kafka.[50]

Yet Muir's own point of view is different: rather than looking at man and the "powers" above him, he sees man and the world about him. The difficulties of day-to-day life had become more apparent to Muir, and he passes by thoughts of "salvation" to emphasize Kafka's temporal concerns.

The Trial was published in 1937, being followed the next year by *America*, the English edition of which includes an "Introductory Note" by Muir. His opinion of Kafka is not significantly different from his earlier one although, having read Brod's *Franz Kafka, Eine Biographie* (1937),[51] he is more aware of the relationship between Kafka's work and his life. The critic's use of such biographical material is justified, he writes, because "no imaginative writer chooses his theme; it is chosen for him by the experience which has most deeply affected him. To trace back the inspiration of Kafka's stories to his relations with his father is not to belittle them or to give them a merely subjective validity. The extraordinary thing in Kafka was the profundity with which he grasped that experience and worked it out in universal terms, until it became a description of human destiny in general into which countless meanings at once ambiguous and clear, could be read."[52] Muir continues to think of Kafka as an allegorical writer, for even though *America*, "the happiest of Kafka's stories, is not allegorical; yet there is something semi-allegorical, or at least representative, about the hero, Karl Rossmann. All Kafka's main figures have this quality; they are not mere individuals; they are images of man in conflict with fate. There are various points, or stations in that conflict."[53]

In the pre-1938 criticism Muir takes for granted the idea that Kafka intends to create allegories based on man's spiritual life. Such an attitude is not unreasonable, yet at the same time Muir was writing the poems in *Variations on a Time Theme* (1934) and *Journeys and Places* (1937). Only a few of them are completely allegorical, but the extended metaphors give them a "semi-allegorical" character; and they often concern the differences between man's actual life and man's ideal life. Muir's criticism of Kafka is intimately connected with the ideas and techniques found in his poems of this period.

In 1940 the Muirs translated excerpts from Kafka's diaries,[54] and in the same year Edwin wrote a lengthy essay for *A Franz Kafka Miscellany* (1940): it shows the development of his understanding of Kafka in the decade since he first studied *The Castle*, as well as the relationship between his criticism and his personal life. His religious experience in February 1939 may account for his bluntly stating in 1940 that Kafka "believed in the fundamental tenets of religion, divine justice, divine grace, damnation and salvation; they are the framework of his world. The problem which possesses him is how man, stationed in one dimension, can direct his life in accordance with a law belonging to another, a law whose workings he can never interpret truly, though they are always before his eyes."[55] Muir also asserts that Kafka holds "the dogma of the incommensurability of divine and human law which he adopted from Kierkegaard," and that this "dogma" is the "source of Kafka's humour[,] . . . a comedy of cross-purposes on a grand scale" (*FKM*, 56 - 57). Ten years earlier Muir saw in Kafka the presentation of man's religious problems in far-reaching terms, but without any commitment by the novelist to a religion. With the renewal of his own religious faith, he finds in Kafka a positive belief which he describes in theological terms. Because of this belief, Kafka's hero does not, and need not, understand the divine laws which govern him; and the novelist's realization of this truth makes life bearable and brings "gleams of pure humour" into the "nightmare atmosphere" of *The Castle* and *The Trial* (*FKM*, 61).

Muir continues to use the word *allegory* for "the form into which

[Kafka] threw his two great religious narratives "(*FKM*, 66), but he stresses the imaginative invention in the novels rather than their symbolism. Studying their plots, he emphasizes that Kafka's humor "can only be shown by showing how he manages the action of his stories." Finding that "every action is perfectly reasonable" (*FKM*, 57, 58), he points out that

Kafka's most ordinary scenes have a fullness which gives them simultaneously several meanings, one beneath the other, until in a trivial situation we find an image of some universal or mythical event such as the Fall. That is the way in which his allegory works. He has been blamed for confusing the two worlds, for introducing real people and then by a sudden twist making all their actions symbolical and bringing them into contact with mythical figures. But that was exactly what he set out to do. Pure allegory could not have expressed his conception of life or his idea of man's moral problem. His hero does not have to walk a beaten road like Christian in *The Pilgrim's Progress*, overcoming set dangers, refusing set temptations, and after each victory drawing nearer to his destination. He did not deny that this road existed; but he found it very hard to distinguish (*FKM*, 59).

Thus while "Bunyan's allegory is a kind of demonstration," Kafka's "is rather an investigation which is both urgent and dramatic, for on its outcome depends the hero's salvation" (*FKM*, 60). Such "action . . . is a sort of dialectic, a progression from one position to the next. The final position, since it is not in this life, is unattainable, and so the allegory can never be finished" (*FKM*, 66). This "allegory" gives more "than the traditional symbols of religion, or than a new interpretation of them" and indeed, "the imaginative logic of the narrative builds up a particularized system of relations which exist by their own right. Kafka's world did not take shape in obedience to these traditional symbols. He arrived at them by mere observation of life as he saw it" (*FKM*, 61). In 1930 Muir emphasizes the similarities between Bunyan and Kafka; in 1940 he sees that Bunyan's allegory is a strict framework imposed from without, while Kafka's is in a sense organic, developing with the action of the story. Not only does Muir understand Kafka's particular type of symbolism more clearly, but he is also more conscious of Kafka's artistry: the novelist's "temper," he writes, "is throughout that of an honest, unassuming workman; he measures and puts together his metaphysical world with the painstaking thoroughness of a mason building a house both to be worked and to be lived in" (*FKM*, 65).

Muir's last study of Kafka was first printed in Czech in the commemorative volume *Franz Kafka a Praha* (1947) and then in English in Muir's *Essays on Literature and Society* (1949).[56] In it his critical attitude is almost directly opposed to that which he held in 1930 and corresponds with the mature concept of life found in his later poetry. He passes over his earlier estimate of the novelist as a thinker beset by religious problems to deal with him as "a great story teller." Kafka always "starts with a general or universal situation" which, being "story-less," forces him to make up the story he tells. "No foundation in fact, no narrative framework, no plot or scene for a plot is there to help him; he has to create the story, character, setting and action, and embody in it his meaning" (*ELS*, 120). Muir's earlier attention to Kafka's plots here reaches its logical conclusion, for the critic considers the novels solely as narratives.

Again Muir brings in the metaphor which he uses so frequently in his poems: "The image of a road," he writes, "comes into our minds when we think of [Kafka's] stories; for in spite of all the confusions and contradictions in which he was involved he held that life was a way, not a chaos, that the right way exists and can be found by a supreme and exhausting effort, and that whatever happens every human being in fact follows some way, right or wrong" (*ELS*, 121). He gives little attention to the external forces which influenced Kafka, for by 1947 his critical practice was to treat a literary work as an entity within itself. Thus while Kafka's understanding of "the irreconcilability of the divine and the human law" was "confirmed" by Kierkegaard, yet Kafka "must himself have made that reading independently"; and, indeed, "the supreme originality of Kafka's work does not lie in his reading of the universal position, which he shared with Kierkegaard at some points, but in his story-telling, by means of which he created a world" and "endlessly surprising" inventions. "The scenes and figures and conversations seem to rise out of nothing, since nothing resembling them was there before. We contemplate them as we contemplate things which we see for the first time" (*ELS*, 122 - 23). Kafka "resurrected and made available for contemporary use the timeless story, the archetypal story, in which is the source of all stories."[57] Finally, in almost direct opposition to the ideas he held for more than fifteen years, Muir writes, "these stories are not allegories. The truths they bring out are surprising or startling, not conventional and expected, as the truths of allegory tend to be. They are more like serious fantasies; the spontaneous expression of Kafka's genius was fantasy, as his early short stories show. . . . But no designation of his art is satisfying. We can see what it was not; to find a name for it is of little consequence" (*ELS*, 124).

One of the least-noticed aspects of the twentieth-century literary scene has been that the influence of modern European writers upon American and English writers has generally been through translations rather than through the original texts. The student of modern literature who concerns himself with such influences must turn to Constance Garnett's Dostoyevsky, to William Archer's Ibsen, Scott-Moncrieff's Proust, and Willa and Edwin Muir's Kafka. The Muirs' place among modern translators is secure not merely because of the quality of their translations but also because of the range. They translated popular novels and biographies which they did not hesitate to rewrite and improve (as comparison of the German and English versions of *Jew Süss* or *Eleanora Duse* shows), while for Broch's and Kafka's novels they scrupulously attempted to understand the writer's aims and to achieve them in English. This translating, whether of masterpieces or of potboilers, influenced Muir by providing him with firsthand information for critical essays and, not infrequently, by reinforcing his intuitive speculations. That the ideas he had attempted to express were integral to the philosophy of respected German writers made it easier for him to continue along ways unfamiliar to contemporary British authors. In addition, the *angst* so obvious in many of these novels forced him to face the Zeitgeist and to consider topics and attitudes which his contemplative, meditative nature might otherwise have allowed him to ignore. J. R. Watson in his essay "Edwin Muir and the Problem of Evil" maintains that Muir "shared the same cultural background with many German thinkers, and fostered it through his work on European writers. Through them, Muir escapes from what he calls the 'provincialism' of Scottish literature; he connects in his own work the seriousness of the Scottish tradition with the seriousness of a writer like Kafka, so that we find in Muir's work a preoccupation with the fundamental questions of the human condition which extends the Scottish tradition and links it with the European."[58] Although Watson may have overestimated this influence, the cumulative effect upon Muir of translating and discussing these European authors is not to be denied; and the translations have a significant place in Edwin Muir's development as a thinker and poet.

CHAPTER 3

The Literary Critic and Essayist

W HILE I have separated the journalism Edwin Muir wrote from his literary writings in order to bring his enormous output of prose into manageable proportions, the distinction also acknowledges his preeminence as a poet and literary critic rather than as a journalist. His journalism should not be ignored, however, because writing for the larger reading public kept him always mindful that his literary essays would be read by many of the same readers and that, if he wished to influence them, he must not alienate himself from them by assuming an overtly highbrow point of view in literary criticism. Predisposed by his religious and political attitudes to the traditional concept that literature should express moral values and make a meaningful comment on life, Muir thus wrote about the modern and avant-garde writers of his time in such a way that his essays were read and appreciated by an extremely large public in England (and by a not inconsiderable number of readers in the United States) and had a very positive influence upon the reception of these writers.

I Latitudes *(1924)*

Although Muir wrote a number of notes on literary matters for *We Moderns,* his first important critical pieces were written after he came to London in 1919. This apprentice work is colored by his preoccupation with modern psychology, for his treatment by the psychologist Dr. Maurice Nicoll helped him solve his personal problems and taught him psychological principles from which he derived what proved to be the appropriate responses to the literature of the day. Catching, as it were, the popular attitude, yet retaining a sense of traditional values, Muir found that editors like John Middleton Murry of the *Athenaeum* were eager to publish his essays, and by January 1921, when Murry published his essay "A Plea for Psychology in

Literary Criticism," the man who less than two years earlier had been an unknown clerk in Glasgow was being published in the company of some of the best-known writers of the day. In these essays for the *Athenaeum*, the *New Age*, and the *Freeman*, Muir developed his aesthetic and philosophical ideas. If there is a lack of agreement among these essays, it is because they are the reflection of Muir's rapidly growing artistic awareness. The majority of them are to be found in *Latitudes* (1924), Muir's first collection of essays, although a number remain uncollected and must be read in their place of original publication. About one-third of the *Latitudes* essays are on literary subjects; the others concern aesthetics, morals, and psychology; and there is also a long essay on Prague and a section of aphorisms and short critical notes similar in form to those in *We Moderns*. Michael Hamburger describes "the Muir of these essays and aphorisms" as "an *esprit fort*, a sophisticated, cynical, utterly individualistic transvaluator of all values—in short, a Nietzschean."[1] Although Hamburger's estimate is generally true, there is actually less mention of Nietzsche in *Latitudes* than in *We Moderns;* and, in fact, in the "Note on Friedrich Nietzsche," a review-essay centered on Janko Lavrin's *Nietzsche and the Modern Consciousness* (1922), Muir attempts to evaluate his response to the philosopher. He had progressed far enough from his former, absolute dependence to recognize Nietzsche's "self-deceptions" and to concede, regretfully, that "we shall probably have to throw away half the more systematic part of Nietzsche's thought"; yet, he goes on, "how much poorer our vision of life to-day would be had Nietzsche never written about Christianity, morality and the Superman. He brought a new atmosphere into European thought, an atmosphere cold, glittering and free; and any thinker in our time who has not breathed in it has, by that accident, some nuance of mediocrity and timidity which is displeasing."[2]

The *Freeman* essays were designed for a free-thinking audience which, though not anticlerical, liked the titillation of attacks on religious institutions; and hence Muir often stresses his antireligious sentiments, exposing the "priests who, whatever their virtues, sin enough to have a little knowledge of psychology, [and who] know that it is never their truths but their seriousness which convinces the masses. In consequence—it is a piece of worldly wisdom which deserves the highest admiration—they have exalted seriousness if not to an art, to a technique, by means of which they can be more apocalyptically and successfully serious than any other human organization" (*L*, 232). These witty half-truths characterize the philosophical essays in the volume, which bear such provocative titles as "The Affirmation of Suffering" and "Against the Wise" and—an obvious gambit for the "youthful" American audience—"In Defense of New Truths."

The essays on literary subjects reflect Muir's current reading, his study of George Douglas resulting from his encounter with *The House with the Green Shutters* (1901). The events of the novel, particularly the prolonged death of the mother, were so similar to happenings in Edwin's own early life that detached criticism loses out to an emotional response. Muir considers the novel to be "subjective" and "objective" autobiography, reconstructing from young Gourlay's character that of George Douglas. This reconstruction shows Muir's own attitude to the world. Douglas, he writes, "revealed [the] ineluctable vulgarity of existence relentlessly; but inwardly he was appalled by it. This much is sure: only a spirit of the most fine fastidiousness could have apprehended vulgarity so vividly and have hated it so extravagantly. The cowardice of the world, the good sense of the average sensual man, may easily see in such an excess of sensitiveness something pathological; but any one who detaches himself from the conspiracy of mankind will scarcely deny that Douglas spoke the truth" (*L*, 38 - 39). Muir forgets his new-found psychology and makes Douglas into the ideal figure of his own time of personal trial, the Nietzschean Superman. He wrote this essay while living in central Europe with no access to biographical information about Douglas (whose life and character were quite unlike Muir's "reconstruction" of them), and his subjective estimate of the novelist indicates how deeply entrenched his Nietzschean beliefs were.

"A Note on Scottish Ballads" is perhaps Muir's most accomplished essay in *Latitudes*. Muir sets up two standards to determine literary value and proves that the Scottish ballads meet these requirements. He argues that the language of a work must be a living language at the time of its use and must have a tradition of "pure" speech. Such was the language of Bunyan and Fielding, but not that of Stevenson, "to whom language was a literary medium and nothing more," nor that of Conrad, who achieved "a picturesque display of words, with something unspanned between the sense and the appearance" (*L*, 14). English cannot be the language for a Scots writer, and since it "became the literary language of Scotland there has been no Scots imaginative writer who has attained greatness in the first or even the second rank through the medium of English" (*L*, 13). Similarly a literary work, he declares, must demonstrate a definite view of life inseparable from the language. Knox, for example, "expressed the national temper when, disdainfully asserting that the image of the Madonna was only 'a bit painted wuid,' he threw it into the sea" (*L*, 16). The language of the ballads was living when they were written and clearly conveyed the "simple vision of life" that sets the Scottish ballads apart from all other ballads and folksongs. English ballads show the philosophy of reflective poetry and the inescapable morality of their singers; but the Scottish ballads are distinguished by "preeminently this sense of immediate love, terror, drama; this ecstatic living in passion at the moment of its expression and not on reflection, and the experiencing of it therefore purely, as unmixed joy, as complete terror, in a concentration on the apex of the moment, in a shuddering realization of the moment . . ." (*L*, 21). Their secret is that "this world in which there is no reflection, no regard for the utility of action, nothing but pure passion seen through pure vision, is, if anything is, the world of art. To raise immediate passion to poetry in this way . . . without the necromancy of memory, requires a vision of unconditional clearness, like that of a child; and it may be said of the Scottish ballad-writers that they obtained poetry by pure, unalleviated insight. . . . [I]n the greatest of the Scottish ballads there is this quality, and this alone. This, and not the occasional strangeness of their subject matter, is what gives them their magic . . ." (*L*, 22 - 23). Muir does not stop at defining a work but rather takes it to be a manifestation of the source behind all similar works; the source here is the Scottish "vision" which passed away forever with the Reformation. Characteristically Muir ignores the questions which the student might pose—the authorship of the ballads, or the authenticity of their texts. Such pedantry was of no interest to him, for he had a more immediate, personal interest in the ballads, that of a poet who was himself trying to find a language in which to express his ideas and who was indeed seeking a vision that would illuminate his poems.

Even though the *Latitudes* essays often concern avant-garde subjects and attitudes, they are composed within the framework and in the terms of the appreciative, nineteenth-century general or belle-lettrist essay and are the direct result of Muir's rapidly increasing intellectual confidence and knowledge. Many of them provide interesting examples of psychological criticism and show the critic's divided allegiance between a Nietzschean ideal and a more realistic, psychological concept of man, while the concern with literature as an expression of the human spirit more than compensates for the sometimes limited factual knowledge.

II   Transition *(1926)*

While Muir was writing for the *Freeman*, he was also contributing reviews, essays, and commentaries to the *New Age;* and when both journals ceased publication, he sent his work to such periodicals as the newly founded *Saturday Review of Literature*, to both the English and American *Nation*, to the *New Republic*, the *Calendar of Modern Letters*, the *Adelphi*, and others. His reviews were generally of con- temporary fiction, while his essays were considerations of either the German writers whom he was currently reading or the contemporary British writers who were experimenting with new forms of expression. He wrote about the latter in a series of essays for the London *Nation* (the New York *Nation* also published them) which he collected—along with a few other essays—in the volume *Transition, Essays on Contemporary Literature* (1926). This collection is almost the only study of experimental, innovative literature published in England between 1920 and 1926 which consistently shows neither false valuations nor a reluctance to pronounce judgments on contem- poraries. Muir's subjects are (with the exception of "Stephen Hud- son") the writers who are today thought of as the most important of that age: James Joyce, D. H. Lawrence, Virginia Woolf, Aldous Hux- ley, Lytton Strachey, T. S. Eliot, Edith Sitwell, and Robert Graves. There are also three essays on "The Zeit Geist," "Contemporary Poetry," and "Contemporary Fiction."

"The Zeit Geist" reflects the critical principles upon which Muir relied when he selected the subjects of his essays. The artist "who ap- prehends the power of the age," he writes, "will regard himself as its enemy" because "all great writers are of their time, though they sometimes think of themselves as outside and against it; and when they attain expression in art the age is interrogating itself, is being differentiated for the purpose of self-realization. Without this hostili- ty against itself the spirit of no age could come to realization; it would remain undifferentiated and unawakened; it could never be objec- tified, for all objectification implies separation."[3] He decides that writers can be classified according to the treatment of the Zeitgeist: the majority, he declares, give "mere expressions of the thing of which as artists they should be the contemplators" and accept "the spirit of the age both consciously and unconsciously; their conscious is accord- ingly a mere passive reflection of a general unconscious, and is in- capable of being turned back into that unconscious, to discover and objectify what is there" (*T*, 6 - 7). In the minority are writers who either struggle with the Zeitgeist or escape from it. Muir prefers the writer who struggles, for only the Zeitgeist of the present gives sufficient resistance "to evoke [the writer's] full powers." The "good writer is not concerned with the things which in literature have been proved permanent, but rather with the things in his age and his experience which have not been so proved, to which by realizing and objectifying them he may give permanence" (*T*, 8).

Considering "disillusionment" to be part of the contemporary Zeitgeist, Muir suggests that the readers of Aldous Huxley may "assume his disillusionment, take it for granted as comfortably as we take any habitual assumption. But when disillusionment is objectified as it is in *Ulysses*, we can no longer do this; we are compelled to reckon with it. We are not at liberty to adopt it as it stands; for this disillusionment is no longer an attitude, but rather all that an attitude by its nature hides and keeps us from seeing. To accept it is not thus to accept another disguise or defence; it is rather to accept in some measure ourselves" (*T*, 12 - 13). Huxley exemplifies the "fashionable writer," and Joyce, the writer who struggles with the Zeitgeist. On the other hand, Lawrence is "the grand example in our age of the poet of escape" who "has brought a profound criticism to bear upon [the age]. His values, his symbols, his hopes, are so opposed at every point to the spirit of the age that he makes us question not one or two, but all of its assumptions. The defect of the literature of escape is that it is too sweeping; it has neither the exactitude nor the practical temper of the literature of conflict" (*T*, 14 - 15). Thus Muir decides that "all the important writers of our time belong to these two categories" of "conflict" or "escape" and that "the rank of these writers will be determined by the thing which at present determines their value for us: the profundity, comprehensiveness and truth of their criticism of contemporary life" (*T*, 15 - 16). The worth of Muir's principles is proved by the fact that the essays in *Transition* continue to be useful interpretations of the respective writers, limited only by the fact that Muir was considering only a small part of the total production of the writers.

For D. H. Lawrence and James Joyce Muir had an almost complete literary oeuvre to consider, and these essays today require few apologies. Muir turns his back on Lawrence's flaunting of sexual conventions, realizing that Lawrence's "spirit is exalted only when it takes fire from his senses; his mind follows the fluctuations of his desires, intellectualizing them, not operating in its own right. But his senses can be set alight by anything natural" (*T*, 49). Muir sees that "action arises in [Lawrence's] novels when the instinctive field of one character impinges on that of another, producing something like an electric shock. . . . Thus Fate . . . is not woven by character, but by instincts which colour character, and sometimes seem independent of it" (*T*, 54). Having stressed in earlier essays the importance of man's being his own master, Muir necessarily finds that Lawrence "has little appreciation of the mind, the soul and character, in themselves. He shows us one marvellous province of life, but not, like the great artists, life itself" (*T*, 59). Although Muir realizes the value of Lawrence's work and the fact that Lawrence "has written in almost all his books more greatly than any other English writer of his time," he sees that "Mr. Lawrence's theories are encroaching on his art, and pushing it out," and suggests that "his art has never attained clarity in itself, and therefore something possessing clarity had to be set alongside it to illumine it. . . . Mr. Lawrence has not brought his art to its perfection; and he theorizes because there is something which he cannot see clearly enough to describe" (*T*, 61 - 63). The vital quality of this criticism comes from a rigid exclusion of all merely temporal concerns and from Muir's going directly to the most distinctive feature in Lawrence's vision: the equation of man's instincts and senses with his rational qualities.

Lacking the vast body of critical information which the present-day student of Joyce can fall back upon, but free from the notion that Joyce can only be read by academics, Muir inevitably writes a general study of Joyce. This essay shows his different attitudes to the British and American publics. In the first part of the essay, originally published in the English *Calendar of Modern Letters*, he controls the language and makes little use of psychological terms.[4] In the second part, written for the American *New Republic*, he expresses the most advanced psychological ideas of the time, even though his language is that of effusive nineteenth-century "appreciations."[5] In the *Calendar* essay he demonstrates Joyce's artistic development from the realistic description of *Dubliners* to "the mastery of language" in *A Portrait of the Artist* without which "*Ulysses* could never have been written" (*T*, 20 - 21). Like almost all critics of the decade, he compares Joyce to Rabelais, declaring that *Ulysses* is less a psychological study than a comedy on the scale of *Gargantua and Pantagruel* in which Joyce destroys the old order, the "weight of second-rate sentiment and thought," in order to make a fresh start (*T*, 32).

Muir alludes to the Jungian theory of the racial unconscious, but not wishing to antagonize his British readers with aggressively new, mid-European words, he employs neutral terms: "Mr. Joyce's prostitutes in the brothel scene . . . are . . . figures in a folk-lore which mankind continually creates, or rather carries with it; creations and types in the dream in which sensual humanity lives, and which to humanity is the visible world. . . . [F]rom it literature arose, for like literature, it is aesthetic, and has the freedom of perception which can only come when men are delivered from their utilitarian prejudices. And to it accordingly literature must periodically come back, as much to test as to renew itself" (*T*, 32 - 33). Thus Joyce's true accomplishment is the transformation of reality into art; the act takes place at times before the reader, so that he sees both the reality and Joyce's transformation of it. In the second part of the essay, Muir describes this process in psychological terms: Joyce, he declares, "has described clearly for the first time the realm only half-glimpsed by writers such as Mr. D. H. Lawrence, Mr. Sherwood Anderson and Miss Dorothy Richardson. He has revealed the swarming world of sub-conscious and half-conscious thoughts which constitute three-fourths of our life, and he has shown that it has a magical and excessive beauty. . ." (*T*, 42 - 43). Throughout Muir holds an uncompromisingly modern point of view, praising *Ulysses* almost without qualifications.

Although the essay on Virginia Woolf seems almost dutifully respectful (she was, after all, the wife of his editor at the *Nation*), Muir wrote in a private letter to Sydney Schiff that "after reading everything she has written I have really a great admiration and respect for her; and I could put all my heart into the essay."[6] Muir seems not to have cared much for Lytton Strachey; and so he diplomatically ignores Strachey's psychological speculations in order to stress the biographer's concern with form. Personal regard for Aldous Huxley and Sydney Schiff ("Stephen Hudson") perhaps influences the treatment of their writings; yet even for his friends Muir carefully qualifies his praise.

In the essays "Contemporary Poetry" and "Contemporary Fiction" Muir stresses the idea that literature reflects society and that the social changes and the breakdown of traditions in the twentieth century have made the writer more necessary than ever before, since life can only be understood when it has been interpreted by the creative artist. The role of the poet is especially difficult, for this is an age of scientific prose; and writers have come to examine life impersonally, "coldly, and involuntarily, automatically so" (*T*, 180). Most of the characters in contemporary fiction cannot communicate with one another, and indeed "the general tendency of the novel at present might be described as anti-humanistic" (*T*, 216). In this remark lies

Muir's primary attitude in this period: he is a humanist writing under the influence of a psychological theory which attempts to account for all of man's activities. In the 1920s man and his temporal problems were at the center of Muir's vision of life; consequently he approved of Mrs. Woolf, who had a similar vision, and felt uneasy before Huxley's strong and one-sided scorn, and before Eliot's unpleasant and unanswered questions. Muir asks that a writer probe into man's psyche as deeply as possible and—equally important—that he resolve and integrate what he finds there. The essays in *Transition* are unified by this critical attitude which, expressed or implied, underlies all of Muir's critical writing at this time.

III   The Structure of the Novel *(1928)*

The Structure of the Novel has probably had more readers and more influence than any other of Muir's critical writings, for it has remained in print, on both sides of the Atlantic, almost continuously since Muir wrote it for the "Hogarth Lectures" series. Muir appears to have studied Percy Lubbock's *The Craft of Fiction* (1921) and E. M. Forster's *Aspects of the Novel* (1927) before beginning to write his essay, for in several ways he specifically reacts to the critical biases of these writers. Indeed their authoritarian tone may well have caused Muir's open iconoclasm: "My concern," he writes, "will not be at all with what . . . plots 'should be,' but simply with what they are. The only thing which can tell us about the novel is the novel."[7] Consciously breaking away from conventional modes of criticism and yet needing some sort of divisions or categories, Muir formulates three main divisions for prose fiction, labeling them the character novel, the dramatic novel, and the chronicle. He describes, rather than defines, these three divisions, his descriptions being perhaps his most original criticism of the novel form. In general, the character novelist tries "to delineate character . . . in such variety as to suggest a picture of society," while the dramatic novelist is concerned with showing "the complete human range of experience in the actors themselves" and the effect of one upon the other (*SN*, 32, 60). The writer of the chronicle creates a segment of time valid for all time. Two lesser divisions of the novel are the novel of action (a series of adventures or stories) and the period novel (a representation of one time in all its particularities).

Muir arrives at these descriptions by studying the plots of various novels. and he gives so much attention to plot and related matters that he fails to consider other aspects of the novel. He defends his emphasis upon plot because "such terms as 'pattern,' 'rhythm,' 'surface,' 'point of view,' and so on" are "controversial or semi-controversial" and "question-begging" (SN, 14, 15). They are also, not incidentally, the most significant terms in Lubbock's and Forster's studies. But *plot*, Muir maintains, "is a definite term, it is a literary term, and it is universally applicable. It can be used in the widest popular sense. It designates for everyone, not merely for the critic, the chain of events in a story and the principle which knits it together"; and thus Muir studies "the lines along which events move in the novel" in order to find the "interior principle" of each novel (SN, 16, 17).

There are two obvious weaknesses in this argument. Although Muir's deductions seem quite reasonable, their validity is directly related to the number and similarity of novels considered, for Muir refers primarily to only a small number of nineteenth-century novelists: mainly Scott, Austen, Thackeray, and Dickens. A further problem results from the all-inclusive nature of his categories: the descriptions of the dramatic novel and the character novel can apply equally well, depending on one's point of view, to the same novel. Realizing this latter weakness and attempting to differentiate between the two types, Muir explains:

The plot of the character novel is expansive, the plot of the dramatic novel intensive. The action of the first begins with a single figure, as in *Roderick Random*, or with a nucleus, as in *Vanity Fair*, and expands towards an ideal circumference, which is an image of society. The action of the second, on the contrary, begins never with a single figure, but with two or more; it starts from several points on its circumference, which is a complex, not a nucleus, of personal relationships, and works towards the centre, towards one action in which all the subsidiary actions are gathered up and resolved. The novel of character takes its figures, which never change very much, through changing scenes, through the various modes of existence in society. The dramatic novel, while not altering its setting, shows us the complete human range of experience in the actors themselves. There the characters are changeless, and the scene changing. Here the scene is changeless, and the characters change by their interaction on one another. The dramatic novel is an image of modes of experience, the character novel a picture of modes of existence (SN, 59 - 60).

Each type of novel must obey its own laws and observe the limitations of its type in order for the writer to "get his effect and externalise his peculiar vision of life" (SN, 61).

The chapter entitled "Time and Space" ostensibly allows Muir to define the "chronicle," but it actually results from his handling similar subjects in his poetry of the late 1920s. His thesis here "is that the imaginative world of the dramatic novel is in Time, the imaginative world of the character novel in Space. In the one . . . Space is more or less given, and the action is built up in Time; in the other, Time is assumed, and the action is a static pattern, continuously redistributed and reshuffled, in Space" (*SN*, 62 - 63). Time is stationary in the character novel, but in the dramatic novel it moves swiftly. Indeed "this urgency of time in the dramatic novel is one of its essential characteristics" (*SN*, 70). Such phrases also characterize the poems Muir was composing at this time, for whether he was writing literary criticism or lyrical verse, his mode of thought is essentially the same. Here these terms allow him to define the "chronicle" as a story that takes place in both time and space. "In *War and Peace*," he writes, "space and time seem equally real; . . . but in fact its action takes place in time and time alone. The houses, the drawing-rooms, the streets, the country estates . . . alter, like the characters, and altering become mere aspects of time" (*SN*, 95). In the dramatic novel the speed of time is psychological; and the contrast between it and the "arithmetical, external aspect of time" gives additional pathos and depth (*SN*, 101). But in the chronicle time has "a cold and deadly regularity, which is external to the characters and unaffected by them. . . . [T]ime is not measured by human happenings, no matter how important; it is; and it continues to exist unchanged after its story has been told, still as regular in its movement, still as rich in accident and in the multitudes of figures it will discover. . . . [W]e see human life as birth, growth, and decay, a process perpetually repeated. This then is the framework, ideal and actual, of the chronicle; its framework of universality" (*SN*, 98, 102 - 103).

Aware that the introduction of "the concepts of Time, Space, and Causality into a work of criticism" may be thought "arbitrary and fanciful," Muir defends himself by arguing that man sees the world in such terms: "[T]he imagination," he declares, "desires to see the whole unity, or an image of it; and it seems that that image can only be conceived when the imagination accepts certain limitations, or finds itself spontaneously working within them. If the matter could be pursued to the end, then I hold that it would be found that those limitations determine the principle of structure in the various types of imaginative creation; in the dramatic novel, for example, the character novel, and the chronicle" (*SN*, 113).

The only mention of contemporary literature occurs in the chapter on "The Period Novel and Later Developments." The period novel shows "a section of contemporary society . . . in transition. . . . It does not try to show us human truth valid for all time; it is content with a society at a particular stage of transition, and characters which are only true in so far as they are representative of that society. It makes everything particular, relative and historical" (*SN*, 116 - 17). Bennett, Wells, Galsworthy, and Dreiser wrote period novels, and their "bondage . . . degraded" the form and "falsified for a time the standards of criticism" because "exactitude of contemporary detail became more important than exactitude of imagination" (*SN*, 118). Proust combines all three types of the novel, while Joyce attempts "to transcend the divisions of the novel," to catch the flux of life, and to employ a symbolism providing additional significance (*SN*, 129 - 30).

The value of *The Structure of the Novel* is due less to Muir's setting up these categories (which do not often help one to reach judgments within the proposed, critical framework) than to Muir's maintaining that the novel has a valid, independent life—"the novel is a form of art, . . . or it is nothing," he declares—and to his questioning why each novel is created in its particular form (*SN*, 150). Muir won his place in the front ranks of the most advanced critics of his time by his willingness to accept new ideas; and the popularity of *The Structure of the Novel* shows the continuing value of his liberal attitude.

IV   Scott and Scotland *(1936)*
and Other Writings on Scottish Literature

One of the effects of the Muirs' sojourn on the Continent and of their work with German novelists was that Edwin and Willa realized that their allegiance was not so much to Scotland (or, even less, to England) as to Europe, and that spiritually and temperamentally they belonged to the European cultural tradition. Muir's convictions on this subject were so strong that in 1934 he and his friend Janko Lavrin edited and published four issues of a literary journal which they named the *European Quarterly*. Although the *Quarterly* allowed them to express political and philosophical ideas which few other contemporary editors shared, and its uncompromisingly serious, advanced attitude was, at least on Muir's part, a reaction to the popular journalism he was forced to write, it was nevertheless intended primarily to "foster the growth of the European spirit in every sphere of human activity. All that it hopes for is to help a little towards the realization of that spirit; and that is its sole policy."[8] Lavrin and Muir published translations of many European writers, being among the first editors to put the work of Federico García Lorca and Søren Kierkegaard before the English-reading public. Being concerned almost daily with the problems of translation and with the relationship of language and national expression, Muir realized that a writer's thought is inextricably involved not only with the specific language which the writer uses, but also with the entire cultural heritage associated with that language.

Because of this understanding Muir had little sympathy with the literary aims of the Scottish Nationalist party, and particularly with Hugh MacDiarmid's notion of "synthetic Scots" or "Lallans"—a language composed of obsolete terms, dialect words, and other remnants of the Scottish language (which, by the twentieth century, had been reduced to various dialects)—a language which was employed only in literary expression and had no connections, either social or literary, with human life.[9] Muir's attitude became more obvious to his fellow Scots when he returned to Scotland in the mid-1930s, particularly in 1935 when he affronted many Nationalists by stating in the "Silver Jubilee Supplement" of the *Scotsman* that the Nationalist movement was really no more than the recognition of the tendency of contemporary Scottish writers to write about the local scene for Scottish rather than English readers.[10] A year later his comments in *Scott and Scotland* (1936) were taken to mark his complete defection from the movement.

Yet London editors thought of Muir as a Scottish specialist and often gave him books about Scotland to review. His first writings for the *Spectator* generally had to do with Scotland, and he used many of these essays in *Scott and Scotland*. Thus his 1932 essay on Sir Walter Scott, occasioned by the centenary of Scott's death and the publication of biographies by John Buchan and Donald Carswell, states the idea developed in *Scott and Scotland* that the novelist was a creator of "solid" minor characters who could not "create a world for them to live in. . . . [He] provided pasteboard."[11] In his 1934 review of *A Book of Scottish Verse* Muir comments on the "narrow limits" of Scottish poetry and the contrast between pre- and post-sixteenth-century Scottish verse, two major themes of the later study.[12] An essay written for the *Modern Scot* in 1932 entitled "Scott and Tradition" clearly states that tradition means the English novel tradition, in which "Scott marks a definite degeneration. . . . [A]fter him certain qualities are lost to the novel which are not recovered for a long time."[13] These essays and reviews show Muir's increasing impatience with the idea of reviving a Scottish literary tradition.

Scott and Scotland is the final volume in a series entitled "Voice of Scotland." The other writers attempt to regenerate the national spirit and are openly friendly to the aims of the Nationalists. In contrast, Muir suggests his negative attitude by presenting in the first two-thirds of his book a wide-ranging history of Scottish literature drawn from M. M. Gray's anthology *Scottish Poetry* (1935) and G. G. Smith's *Scottish Literature: Character and Influence* (1919); the last third concerns Sir Walter Scott. Only the seven-page "Conclusions" is akin to the critical, prescriptive tone of the other books in the series.

Muir also writes about the relationship of language and literature. Using Scotland as his specific example, he decides that until approximately 1600 Scottish writers used a single language for day-to-day life and writing, and that after 1600 they employed English for their serious writing, while Scots remained their spoken language and, indeed, the language in which they thought. But "the prerequisite of an autonomous literature is a homogeneous language," Muir declares, for it is "the only means yet discovered for expressing the response of a whole people, emotional and intellectual, to a specific body of experience peculiar to it alone, on all the levels of thought from discursive reason to poetry. And since some time in the sixteenth century Scotland has lacked such a language."[14] Thus, "reduced to its simplest terms, this linguistic division means that Scotsmen feel in one language and think in another." Scots dialect is associated with "local sentiment," while "standard English . . . is almost bare of associations other than those of the classroom" (SS, 21). Yet another reason for the poverty of Scottish poetry is its lack of dramatic antecedents. Thus Muir questions whether Scottish poetry can be said to provide "a satisfactory tradition for a native poet" (SS, 118). He turns to Scott, declaring that he was "by instinct a conservative who believed in the established order and tradition. . . . The established order was the Union, and . . . he had no choice but to adhere to it; for it was rooted in history and sanctified by the past. But at the same time he saw this established order gradually destroying another established order, that of Scotland. That order was equally old, equally rooted in history and sanctified by the past, and moreover it was the order to which he was most intimately bound by birth, early memory and the compulsion of his imagination" (SS, 114 - 15). Scott's language parallels that of other native writers. "Where he wished to express feelings of more than ordinary seriousness and range, or feelings modified by thought, he employed English, using Scots for the simplest purposes of humour and pathos" (*SS*, 174).

Thus Muir decides that "the Scots language as a vehicle for literature, . . . the Scottish literary tradition, [and] . . . the political and social state of Scotland" are all "unsatisfactory bases . . . for a genuinely autonomous literature" (*SS*, 176). Scottish writers must resolve to absorb the English literary tradition and henceforth write in English. Modern Irish writers provide a precedent; and their nationality, Muir observes, "cannot be said to be any less intense than ours" (*SS*, 179). In part Muir bases his concepts of language and national identity on theories of the racial unconscious, his specific judgments about Scottish literature probably being influenced by his thesis. Yet, while he came to value Scott more highly than he does here, he never altered his basic concept of Scott's character; and he frequently referred to the difference he saw in pre- and post-Reformation Scottish literature: a few years later he decided that the Reformation is the dividing point between an almost mystical good way of life and the unsatisfactory modern way. *Scott and Scotland* was written as an occasional piece in the context of a literary and political controversy, but it reveals significant developments in Muir's thought.

V   Introductions to English Literature,
Volume Five: The Present Age from 1914 *(1939)*

The most unusual of these literary studies is the volume which Muir wrote for the series entitled *Introductions to English Literature*. Professor Bonamy Dobrée was the general editor, and the authors of the different volumes, with the exception of Muir, were all professors or lecturers at British universities and colleges. Each *Introduction* deals with a historical period, giving a brief survey of its literature and life, as well as selected bibliographies of the writers of the period. The series was designed for general readers (rather than specialized students) who wanted a planned approach to their reading and is further evidence of Dobrée's interest in adult education. Obviously such scholarly work was unlike anything Muir had previously attempted; he was further handicapped by the fact that his wife was seriously ill while he was working on the book; and he had neither the time nor the inclination for such unfamiliar tasks. Had circumstances been different, *The Present Age* might have been successful; but, due both to its shortcomings and to the passage of time which rapidly makes the "present" into the "past," it was withdrawn from the series in 1958 and replaced by David Daiches's *The Present Age from 1920*. Yet none of Edwin Muir's books is completely without merit, and although there are many faults to this one—the bibliographical information, for example, is quite inadequate—some of the survey chapters provide useful information and helpful critical attitudes.

The best chapters are those on "General Background" and "Poetry." In the former Muir emphasizes the connection between literature and life, again describing the twentieth-century disintegration of society, particularly into the opposed forces of capital and labor, pointing out that writers have retreated "into private worlds" because "society [can]not be seen and felt coherently."[15] Yeats and Pound show this "retreat" in their use of the past, while Eliot uses "his own reconstruction" of the order of past things (*PA*, 32). The themes of modern poetry also illustrate this disintegration, for "one public crisis after another" has caused a shift "from a conservative to a revolutionary attitude" (*PA*, 34). Such observations sound like commonplaces today, but in 1939 they were received by the leader writer of the *Times Literary Supplement* as "a valuable diagnosis of a condition which, because it has developed very gradually, tends to escape observation."[16] Muir emphasizes the *angst* of the decade and the relative, becoming quality of time as it appears in modern literature, and he explains postwar experiments in the novel as a result of "the increasing confusion of society": the novelist has no stable society which he can use in his work and is therefore driven to experiment (*PA*, 42).

The poetry chapter is a capable, condensed history of twentieth-century English verse; it is of interest because it contains a straightforward statement of Muir's standards for poetry. He demands a "quality of incontestable greatness," which he defines as "the power to make a natural, immediate and yet overwhelming statement which produces such conviction that we forget the voice that utters it." Such a quality is rare in the poetry written between 1909 and 1939, although "we find it occasionally in Eliot's poetry. . . . We find it too, though less perfectly, in Hopkins, . . . less often in Yeats and hardly at all in Pound" (*PA*, 43 - 44). The terms "natural" and "artificial" apply to the sources of poetry. "Natural" poetry comes fully formed from the poet's unconscious; "artificial," from the poet's controlled mind (*PA*, 47 - 48). Although poetry which the poet has consciously controlled can attain beauty, it will not have the "quality of incontestable greatness." Muir's distinctions appear to depend on the image in the poem and the image evoked in the reader, because he usually finds the desired quality in verses which have a concrete image meaningful to all men, or which evoke such an image. Both types derive from the relatively restricted body of archetypal images. In "The Tower" Yeats's "poetic vision . . . is undeniable; but it is a vision of figures from literature and painting flung into violent movement, and it calls up Shakespeare and Breughel, not the Ireland of which Yeats is writing. The use of language is extremely skilful, and perhaps inspired" (*PA*, 46). Since the appeal of these verses is restricted to readers who know literature and painting, the passage lacks "incontestable greatness." Yeats's "Great Memory" may indeed be the racial unconscious, but the verses are about this source of images; they do not come from it, and Yeats is therefore "artificial" rather than "natural."

The chapter on fiction is an efficient survey of a number of novelists in which some of the judgments are worth remembering as final pronouncements, even though Muir made them after reading only a small part of the writer's output. But the selection of authors is determined to a large extent by Muir's *Listener* reviews; and, because Muir appears never to have decided whether the modern novel in general or only the influential novel was his subject, he frequently falls between the stools of the avant-garde and the best-seller. That the judgments in *The Present Age*, in spite of its faults, are on the whole still valid can probably be laid to Muir's taste and critical principles. As a reviewer in the *Times Literary Supplement* observed, Muir is "cavalier to an extreme. . . . He has his values, and he sticks to them. . . . Intensity which is the excellence of every art . . . is the quality which Mr. Muir pursues."[17] Even though *The Present Age* cannot be used today as a reference book, it is an interesting study of literature by a nonacademic critic, as well as a period piece which faithfully transcribes the feeling of "a menaced world."

VI   Essays on Literature and Society (1949, 1965)

After Muir began working for the British Council in 1942, he wrote fewer essays than in the prewar years, and *Essays on Literature and Society* contains all of his major essays and lectures written between 1939 and 1949. For the second edition Muir revised each essay and added six pieces that he wrote after 1949. The volume includes the W. P. Ker Memorial Lecture, given by Muir at the University of Glasgow in April 1946. Entitled "The Politics of *King Lear*," it illustrates the way in which Muir constantly weaves together his ideas about life, philosophy, and literature. In 1945 he had been appointed director of the British Institute in Prague, and he and Willa had returned to the city they had known in the early 1920s. In the war-torn city he saw how a peaceful way of life had come to an end (his poem "The Good Town" summarizes his attitude); and he became more aware of his concept of man's good life in the past. Looking at *King Lear* he saw it to be a paradigm of the situation that preoccupied him; and he declared in his lecture that "in the interval between [1539 and 1649] the medieval world with its communal tradition was dying, and the modern individualist world was bringing itself to birth." He maintains that

The old world still echoed in [Shakespeare's] ears; he was aware of the new as we are aware of the future, that is as an inchoate, semi-prophetic dream. Now it seems to me that that dream, those echoes, fill *King Lear* and help to account for the sense of vastness which it gives us, the feeling that it covers a far greater stretch of time than can be explained by the action. The extreme age of the King brings to our minds the image of a civilisation of legendary antiquity; yet that civilisation is destroyed by a new generation which belongs to Shakespeare's own time, a perfectly up-to-date gang of Renaissance adventurers. The play contains, therefore, or has taken on, a significance which Shakespeare probably could not have known, and without his being aware, he wrote in it the mythical drama of the transmutation of civilisation.[18]

The evil characters "never feel that they have done wrong . . . because they represent a new idea; and new ideas, like everything new, bring with them their own kind of innocence" (*ELS*, 35). Lear himself represents a kingdom which "exists as a memory and no longer as a fact; the old order lies in ruin, and the new is not an order. The communal tradition, filled with memory, has been smashed by an individualism that exists in its perpetual shallow present" (*ELS*, 49). Muir realizes that this interpretation is closely related to ideas he expresses in his imaginative writings, and he justifies his subjective criticism by maintaining that every critic "must . . . bring to his interpretation of works of imagination not only his reading, but his life, the experiences he has passed through, the emotions he has felt, the reflections he has made upon them, even the accidents and trivialities of every day, since they are all parts of life and help us, therefore, to comprehend the poet's image of life" (*ELS*, 33). This defense of his critical principles explains the most important attributes of Muir's criticism, its universality and its stress upon personal and social values.

This volume contains several essays which were written as early as 1931; and since Muir revised them extensively for republication, the contrast between the early and late versions highlights Muir's final prose style. The essay which best illustrates his development is an appreciation entitled "Laurence Sterne," first published in the American *Bookman* in March 1931.[19] In 1949 he revised individual sentences while retaining the original form of the whole, even to the paragraphing. In the earlier period he often creates highly involved sentences in which the multiple images and side-thoughts sometimes blur the principal idea, and in which the surface excitement of the language seems almost a deliberate mask for the writer's obscured vision. Similes and metaphors are completely worked out, and the rhetoric is labored:

1931	1949
It [the opening] sets the key, and determines the style, of *A Sentimental Journey;* it is irrevocable, like those first bars in a prelude which preordain all the forms into which a musical composition will flow.	It [the opening] sets the key of *A Sentimental Journey,* and is like one of those themes which preordain all the forms into which a musical composition will flow.
It raises us at once to the altitude where during the course of the book we shall be sustained; it has the inexplicable force of an incantation; and yet it is only a sentence of nine short words. . . .	It raises us to the level where the book will stay; it has the force of an incantation. . . .
They [*Tristram Shandy* and *A Sentimental Journey*] stand secure, on a different plane of perfection from all other English works of prose fiction, as complete triumphs of reason and imagination over subject-matter, that old enemy of the artist, some unsubdued vestiges of which are to be found in almost all novels.	They [*Tristram Shandy* and *A Sentimental Journey*] stand on a plane of their own in English fiction, as triumphs of reason and imagination over subject-matter.

In the 1949 revision the generalizations are reduced in scope; and indiscriminate enthusiasm gives way to reserved judgments which are more forceful. Thus the sentence in 1931—"In all other English novels we can complacently separate form and content, treatment and subject-matter; but in these two books they are indivisible; there is no hiatus between intention and fulfilment, no even momentary absence of the utmost finish of skill to give us a glimpse of a writer sweatily wrestling with his material."[20]—becomes in 1949—"In most novels we can roughly separate form and content, treatment and subject-matter; but in these two books they are indivisible; there seems to be no hiatus between intention and execution" (ELS, 50). The compulsion to stress the main points of the argument stands in contrast to the subtle presentation, a difference apparent throughout the two versions of the essay. Muir appears to have been formerly at some distance from the object of his thought and now to have approached closer to it, for the change is due to more than an increased facility with words.

These essays provide typical examples of Muir's style, while the critical judgments represent the knowledge gained through almost thirty years of practical experience. Muir's critical practice cannot be reduced to formulae or even categories, for it is always eclectic and highly idiosyncratic, although such a phrase as "traditionally humanistic" might perhaps describe it. Certainly the first two essays in the collection could be so described, for in "Robert Henryson" and "Royal Man: Notes on the Tragedies of George Chapman" Muir concerns himself primarily with the moral and ethical concepts of the two authors. His appreciation of Henryson is based on his own attitudes to life before the Reformation: Henryson, he writes, "lived near the end of a great age of settlement, religious, intellectual and social; an agreement had been reached regarding the nature and meaning of human life, and the imagination could attain harmony and tranquillity. It was one of those ages when everything, in spite of the practical disorder of life, seems to have its place . . . and the life of man and of the beasts turns naturally into a story because it is part of a greater story about which there is general consent" (ELS, 10). Henryson represents to Muir the order implicit in his own ideal "good life." Similarly in the essay on Chapman Muir evaluates literature as an expression of life. "Chapman," he declares, "is not interested in human nature, or in practical morality, or in evil, but in the man of excessive virtue or spirit or pride" (ELS, 22). Through such men, particularly Bussy d'Ambois and Byron, "we come to know what morality is . . .

to Chapman" (*ELS*, 32). Muir's critical practice is shaped in part by his lack of academic training, and certainly his religious preoccupation motivates his critical concerns; yet his method is vindicated by its success. With only a few references to the ideas of Chapman's time and only an incidental consideration of the plays as dramatic works, he makes Chapman interesting and pertinent to the general reader—to whom the essay was, after all, addressed.

Muir expresses his critical and philosophical principles most fully in "The Natural Man and the Political Man," developing through references to novels a hypothesis concerning the modern concept of man. In the nineteenth century "natural man" is regarded as "capable of betterment, but, unlike the natural man of religion, [as not needing] regeneration." This "natural man . . . follows a natural development from birth to death, and since this is all that is allowed him, it is important that he should pass through all its stages—childhood, adolescence, love, maturity—in a manner closely corresponding to the requirements of nature; otherwise he will be 'frustrated' or 'distorted.' His upbringing, his surroundings, his ideas, should be as 'natural' as possible. If they are, the expectation is that he will turn out to be satisfactory." Because this man is actually "never quite satisfactory," his difficulties are "taken to be due to the imperfection of our political and social system, and under a perfect constitution the assumption is that [they] would disappear." Thus, "the corollary of the natural man is . . . the political man: the man conscious that something must be done collectively by all natural men, or a majority or an effective minority of them, in order that an opportunity may be given to every natural man to develop his natural potentialities in the most natural way conceivable" (*ELS*, 150 - 51). This concept results in "a reduction of the image of man, who has become simpler, more temporal, more realistic and more insignificant" (*ELS*, 151 - 52). Because of this change, Muir writes, "there seem to be only two directions in which [man] can advance: towards Communism or towards Fascism" (*ELS*, 158). Writing in the pro-Russian atmosphere of the early 1940s, he passed over Communism and discussed the more immediate threat of Fascism, particularly as it appears in the writings of D. H. Lawrence and Henri de Montherlant, "who have described the natural man most penetratingly and eloquently [and] are therefore almost of necessity Fascists by implication."[21] Their work is typical of "a general tendency" in literature, "a simplification of the idea of man"; and "only those writers who are deeply rooted in tradition, and possessed with the idea of time, have been able to make headway against it; such writers as Proust, James Joyce and Virginia Woolf" (*ELS*, 161). In 1949 Muir adds to the essay his admission that human life is a development; yet he maintains that political thinkers who base their thoughts upon mechancial evolution are wrong, "for as man is a moral being, human development can be conceived only as a moral development; no evolutionary process can bring us brotherhood and justice" (*ELS*, 162). The revision ends with an appraisal of Wordsworth, who saw that God, man, and nature "interpenetrated one another in innumerable ways":

> The poetry of Wordsworth has the truth of a vision. . . . [I]t records a moment of mystical co-operation between reason and impulse, man and nature; it does not describe a process, or make a general statement about life which can be embodied in a theory. . . . But Wordsworth's followers vulgarised his conception of nature, and reduced to a dogma what to him had been an illumination; and between them with their crude faith in mountains and woods and the evolutionists with their benevolent universe evolving towards even greater benevolence, there was an intellectual and emotional affinity. Both of them, unintentionally, helped to set the moving principle of good outside man, and in doing so helped to dehumanise experience and history; whereas Wordsworth was essentially concerned with the mind of man and its capacity to respond to the mighty sum of things for ever speaking. In the response lay the co-operation between impulse and reason, and the possibility of harmony; without the response there was no harmony, and it could not be created by means of a theory concerning it. But the theory, nevertheless, dominated the nineteenth century, and has extended its influence over ours (*ELS*, 163, 164).

Muir's intuitive philosophy generally finds its most complete expression in poetry, yet its basic outlines are clearly sketched in these essays. They also express Muir's belief that literature primarily reflects man's life, for Muir never radically altered his approach in *We Moderns:* literature is neither solely an aesthetic object nor a mirror of physical reality, but a record of man's spiritual life in all its forms. Muir upholds a traditional way of thinking about man, and although he can be called a subjective critic, his mature outlook on life removes the stigma of the label. He offers no shortcuts to would-be critics, for his criticism comes not only from "a long experience of books, poems, writings of all kinds," but also from a life rich in experiences on both social and personal levels.[22] In his critical essays and lectures he applies the lessons which life taught him.

VII   The Estate of Poetry *(1962)*

The last work to be noticed here is the posthumously published collection of the six lectures which Muir gave at Harvard in 1955 - 1956 while serving as the Norton Professor of Poetry. This appointment, an international recognition of Muir as a poet and critic, was such a fitting climax to his literary career, while the posthumous publication of the lectures culminated so many years of literary criticism, that it would be pleasing to point to the lectures as a summary of Muir's ideas and perhaps even to find in them oracular pronouncements on the nature of poetry and criticism. But like everything else Muir ever wrote or said, they too are part of his total development and hold no surprises for the reader familiar with his work. Indeed in them he generally restates concepts found in his earlier essays, taking his specific examples and analogies from the *Observer* reviews which he wrote between 1950 and 1955.

The general idea in *The Estate of Poetry* (1962) is based on Muir's long-held belief that literature and life must always be considered together and that consequently the critic must study the relationship between the poet and his public and the effect of this public on poetry. In the title lecture Muir uses the Scottish ballads to illustrate the idea he had written about since the early 1930s: that in the past few centuries the organization of man's life changed so drastically that a poet can no longer be in touch with the sources of poetry, the "natural," ordered way of life; and consequently the modern poet is rarely able to rise above his civilization and produce great poetry. But the ballads come from an integrated society in which men, working with the natural sources of the necessities of life, knew their place in the world; and they show "that great poetry can, or once could, be a general possession."[23]

The lecture "Wordsworth: Return to the Sources" is explained by the title: Muir predictably stresses the "Preface" to *Lyrical Ballads*, declaring that the story in a poem makes it more universal. "The tragic story," he writes, "affects us with unique power because it moves in time, and because we live in time. It reminds us of the pattern of our lives; and within that pattern it brings our loves, our passions, their effects, and unavoidable chance" (*EP*, 29). Wordsworth finds the sort of story which returns him to the source of poetry, the earth itself. Muir discusses at length the poem that had always been his favorite, "The Affliction of Margaret," and then turns to the "Intimations Ode." In it, he maintains, "we feel that

[Wordsworth's] imagination has been humanized, and that he has found that resignation which is a form of acceptance" (*EP*, 38). These ideas are closely related to the poetic theory behind Muir's own verse; and indeed, in this lecture and that on Yeats, Muir speaks as much about himself as about his announced topics. Thus he declares that Yeats's prose "is filled with ideas put as rhetorical questions, a great trick of his. The word 'perhaps' recurs persistently, even when he is setting down a thought which, one would have imagined, must have been of the utmost importance to him" (*EP*, 54). Although Muir thought that he was responding to Yeats, he was actually describing his own literary practice, for he of course employed similar rhetorical devices in his poems and prose.

In "Criticism and the Poet" Muir voices his prejudices against analytical critics, preferring those informed, late - nineteenth-century writers (he names Saintsbury, Quiller-Couch, Raleigh, and Grierson, in particular) whose enthusiasm for poetry made them want to write about it and to share their experience with other readers. Poetry, Muir unequivocally states, is an experience to be enjoyed, not a problem to be studied, and the contemporary, methodical study of poetry is in part responsible for the "divorce between the public audience and the poet" (*EP*, 77).

In the last lecture, "The Public and the Poet," Muir looks first at the modern public which wants scientific knowledge and hence finds no use for poetry. Yet poetry, he asserts, also has its object, which is not knowledge in the scientific or philosophical sense, but "the creation of a true image of life" (*EP*, 107). Poetry comes from the imaginative faculty common to all men, and since poetry is "the supreme expression of imagination . . . it has a responsibility to itself: the responsibility to preserve a true image of life. If the image is true, poetry fulfills its end" (*EP*, 108). Such an image can only be formed when life has a recognizable order, and the dilemma of the modern poet is that modern society has lost the order which formerly made it cohesive; the poet, "confronted with an undifferentiated public . . . does not know to whom he is speaking" (*EP*, 106). Yet he must see past the public, or through it, "to the men and women, with their individual lives, who in some strange way and without their choice are part of it, and yet are hidden by it" (*EP*, 110).

VIII *Summary*

The literary studies, reviews, and other commissioned books discussed in this and the preceding chapter form, both in volume and in quality, an impressive body of work. They were almost all well received by the contemporary public, and some of them still find new readers each year. They show that Muir occupies a place in the history of literary criticism midway between the nonacademic journalist and the perhaps overly restricted academic critic. Had his family background been different, he might well have become a professional scholar, for his natural bent was always toward a serious study of literary problems and philosophy.

Muir's prose writings of the 1920s embody a criticism which is directed against contemporary values and critical practices, and which has a place within the general overthrow of older standards that characterized the decade. But Muir was less a revolutionist (like, for example, H. L. Mencken) than a neurotic believer in Nietzsche who also disliked Calvinism; and considering the limited education and cultural background that he brought to his work we may decide that "rebellion" was the only original attitude he could take at this time. Indeed, although his Nietzschean point of view supplies the surface brilliance of the early essays (and distinguishes them from the later essays), their enduring qualities actually come from his innate taste and ability to appreciate works of art. By the end of the 1920s, when he had developed his writing skills and had considerably broadened his cultural awareness (not least through his life in London and on the Continent with Willa Muir), he moved away from such a point of view. He ceased to place a high premium on the new and different and began to write within the forms and styles used by his contemporaries. But he carried over from this period a quality he never lost, a willingness to accept new works of literature on their own merits. This attitude made him the ideal critic of the avant-garde literature of the time, even though as he grew older he increasingly asked that a writer say something of importance about human life, while treating man as an immortal spirit. Muir came to regard literature as a record of man's spiritual life, and he made its fidelity to such a record a criterion of his judgment. Hence, while he was basically receptive to new writings and to new ideas, he insisted on seeing them within the continuum of the humanistic tradition. This ability to view the individual work in terms of the whole literature is a characteristic of some of the greatest critics of the past, and it may in future years prove to be one of the most valuable aspects of Edwin Muir's literary criticism.

CHAPTER 4

The Novelist and Autobiographer

E DWIN Muir was not only an accomplished essayist, literary
critic and reviewer, translator, and biographer, but he was also a
novelist and autobiographer. His novels must be considered alongside
his autobiographies because they too are based on his own experiences. During the years he was writing *The Marionette* (1927),
The Three Brothers (1931), and *Poor Tom* (1932), he wrote very few
poems, his novels serving as the main outlet for both his creative imagination and for explorations of the meaning of his life. When he
achieved the full expression of his personal beliefs in his third novel,
he abandoned prose fiction in favor of poetry. Then, some years later,
he wrote about his life in *The Story and the Fable* (1939) without the
disguises that are found in the novels. Still later he revised and expanded this work, publishing it under the title *An Autobiography*
(1954). The novels are considerable literary achievements, not least
because of the way in which Muir makes such very different stories
out of his personal experiences. The two autobiographies are masterpieces within their genre, and they provide the essential information
which the reader needs for the complete understanding of Muir's
poems.

I   *The Three Novels*

Plot summaries of the three novels help to show the similarities
among what are ostensibly three entirely different works of fiction
and also lead one toward their common source in their author's life.
The setting of *The Marionette* (1927) is modern Salzburg; the two
main characters are a middle-aged widower and his feebleminded
son, Hans. The housekeeper, Emma, takes care of Hans, and Martin
ignores him until she insists that his fourteenth birthday must be
recognized. Martin then attempts to bring the boy out of his vacancy
by gaining his confidence, walking with him and taking him to the

marionette theater. Hans is fascinated by the miniature production of *Faust*, and his father secures the Gretchen marionette for him, which joins his collection of dolls in the dollhouse built on Martin's orders for him. Martin appears to hope that Hans's interest in the little world of the marionettes will awaken in him an interest in or a grasp of the larger world of reality. But the dolls only increase Hans's confusion about himself and reality, and eventually the father realizes that he can do nothing for his son. In the abrupt conclusion the reader is told that Martin becomes reconciled to Hans's condition and that they live out their days happily enough.

The Three Brothers (1931), a *bildungsroman* set in Scotland during the Reformation, is the story of David Blackadder and his relationship with his father, a Renaissance humanist; with his twin-brother, Archie, his "evil genius"; and with his older brother, Sandy, a fanatic Calvinist. David lives on the family farm and is educated by his father; he goes to St. Andrews to study and then to Edinburgh, where he is frustrated in his love affair with Ellen, who is seduced by Archie. Ellen is subsequently murdered by her former fiancé, who also wounds Archie; and Sandy dies of consumption, having renounced Calvinism for the more liberal tenets of the Anabaptists. David frees himself from his twin brother's influence and leaves Scotland for England and the Continent.

Poor Tom (1932) takes place in Glasgow during 1911 - 1913; it is the story of the brothers Tom and Mansie, their mother, Mrs. Manson, and their cousin Jean. The action is slight; indeed, in Chapter Nineteen, an essay on Christianity and socialism, no mention is even made of the story. Mansie, the main character, is disliked by Tom because Mansie has achieved social and business successes beyond Tom's powers and has taken his sweetheart, Helen, from him. Tom begins to drink and injures his head in a fall while drunk. The injury causes a brain tumor, and the second half of the novel is a description of his prolonged illness and eventual death. During his illness Mansie breaks his engagement to Helen and makes a reconciliation with his brother. The last pages of the novel give Mansie's "vision" of the world and of his place therein.

Each novel centers upon one main character, a young man who in spite of apparent differences actually portrays the author. The differences among these three fictional characters reflect the maturing of Muir's personality and the development of his understanding of himself. *The Marionette* was written after the Muirs had lived on the Continent for several years, some months of which had been spent in

Salzburg. In spring 1925 they went to the south of France, where
Muir "began to write [his] story about Salzburg."[1] *The Marionette* is
not a conventional first novel. The *Times Literary Supplement*
reviewer describes it as "a curious book: indeed, one cannot call it a
novel at all, but a *conte* the artistic purpose of which is obscure." The
reviewer praises "the carefulness of the writing, the precision of the
detail, the obvious rhythm, and the completeness of the construction," yet he finds that "the studied objectivity of the presentation
leaves a reader who does not instinctively respond to grope uncertain-
ly for the reason why the emotions and reactions of a half-witted boy
should have any but a pathological importance."[2] Hans, the "half-
witted boy" who is the principal figure, is not actually a *character*, but
rather one aspect of his creator, while his being placed in Salzburg is
determined largely by Muir's wish to introduce the Austrian
landscape and to utilize Salzburg's famous marionette theater. The
latter supplies the "heroine" of the novel, the Gretchen marionette
with whom Hans falls in love.

Between his first and second novels, Muir wrote various prose
works, including *John Knox, Portrait of a Calvinist* (1929). The
historical research which he had to do for this biography proved to
him that the Reformation was the most important influence on contemporary Scottish life and also convinced him that the agrarian life
he had known as a child in the Orkney Islands was typical of life from
time immemorial, that he had indeed lived an archetypal existence
between his birth in 1887 and the removal of his family to Glasgow in
1901. This belief colors much of his later work, including *The Three
Brothers*, in which he describes his childhood in terms of fictional,
sixteenth-century characters. He has no difficulty in placing these
autobiographical events in the time setting of the Reformation, for,
believing that there is no difference between his own time and that of
the sixteenth century, he writes of them without attempting to
recreate a historical period in the style of such a novelist as
Feuchtwanger. With the exception of the melodramatic events of the
second part of the novel, *The Three Brothers* is much the same story as
is found in *An Autobiography*, told there in the first person.

The Three Brothers brought Muir back to his native land, and in his
last novel he considers not merely his own country but his own time as
well: *Poor Tom* takes place in Glasgow during the first decade of the
century and is a barely disguised account of the formation of Edwin
Muir's own social attitudes. While it may well have been influenced
by some of the works which the Muirs had translated—"Ludwig
Renn's" *War* (1929) and *After War* (1931) and Feuchtwanger's *Two*

Anglo-Saxon Plays (1928) deal, for instance, with the awakening of social consciousness—an awareness of politics and society is so much a part of the literature of the time that *Poor Tom* was probably not so much influenced by other works as it is a product of the same Zeitgeist. This contemporaneous quality of *Poor Tom* is found also in *The Three Brothers* and *The Marionette*, an historical novel and a surrealistic fantasy respectively, for each is typical in its kind of its year. Muir attempts in each novel to use a popular form, yet each is so imprinted with his personality that his novel stands out from others of the same type.

All three novels concern approximately the same period of adolescency in the main character's life. Although these three young men—Hans the Austrian idiot, David the sixteenth-century Scotsman, and Mansie the twentieth-century Glaswegian—appear to be dissimilar in character, their real difference comes from the distance at which their creator places them before the reader. Hans, the idiot, is the most removed, since his psychological condition alienates him from even the other characters in the novel. That it was not Muir's intention to portray another "idiot boy" (as Faulkner was to do with his Benjy) can be seen in his inconsistent handling of point of view in relation to Hans, for Hans's abilities vary widely. At times he possesses a poet's vision: "[A] lizard scuttling across the stones would make the place insecure [to Hans]. He saw nature as a terrifying heraldry. The cat, the lizard and the wasp were embattled forces armed for war, carrying terror and death on their blazoned stripes, their stings, claws and tongues. He could only run away from them to the vacancy of his room."[3] And again Hans is like a mystic or seer:

Once when he was with his nursemaid on the crest of the Kapuziner Berg he saw a sight which he remembered always afterwards. The evening was still; the sun was setting behind the mountains; from the town, whose roofs were gilded by the light, came the sound of bells. Beneath him, overhanging a little precipice, lay a sloping bank, very green in the level light, and over it, in silence, three black dogs were coursing. Their snouts tied to the ground, their sides sharpened, their eyes desperate, they flew around in circles. Sometimes their paws spurned clods and stones over the cliff, but they never stopped. Round them the turf glowed, every blade of grass glittered with a vivid, wakening green, but they seemed to have no kinship with it; they were as chill and dark as the mould beneath. Hans knew that the ground had once been a grave, and he had a vision of the spirit, a few feet underground, racing the dogs and maliciously leading them on. When the last rays left the mound all three stopped, tumbled over one another, and leapt round their master, who was sitting near. But Hans was afraid (*M*, 4 - 5).

Yet most often Hans is merely an idiot who may awaken pity, but whose insight is nil and whose apprehension is so worthless that the novelist completely passes it by: "It was too cold for [Hans] to sit in the shed. Accordingly the dolls and the dolls' house were installed in his bedroom, but although he spent all his time there he paid little attention to them. Sometimes he sat mute and vacant; sometimes he walked restlessly to and fro as if seeking release" (M, 58).

In contrast to Hans, David and Mansie are placed very close to the reader. Muir handles the sixteenth-century characters as if they were contemporaries; he mentions historical events and makes dramatic use of them, but The Three Brothers is not a period novel with a detailed reconstruction of a particular time and place. The historical setting is valuable to the novelist mainly because it gives him an objective point of view for handling incidents from his own life. Thus for example David hears his mother speak to the laborer Sutherland:

[O]ne day Mrs. Blackadder burst out on Sutherland when they were all seated at their midday meal, accusing him of having been out again the night before. The twins stopped eating and gazed at him; his face was changing under their eyes and growing grave and important. Now they would know all about it at last, they thought, but Sutherland's words only cast them into deeper perplexity. "I swear on my oath, mistress, that I wasna away from this house all night. I'll no' deny though," he added, as if trying to remember, "that I mightna have been out in the yard in the dawing on a matter of needcessity." Mrs. Blackadder laughed scornfully, and their father said: "Needcessity! Ay, Sutherland, we ken your needcessity." And later, after Sutherland had left, he said, as if to himself: "Why, the man canna look at them, it seems, without them getting in the family way!" It was more than ever a mystery to the twins, and for days afterwards they gazed at Sutherland in respect and wonder, and were a little afraid of him when he joked with them. [4]

The portrait of Sutherland is actually a direct copy of Muir's cousin Sutherland, who lived with the family in the Orkneys. The sketch of him in Muir's An Autobiography is in the same vein as the account in the novel: "His language," Muir writes, "was very free, and his advances shockingly direct, but always with a show of reason. He never tried to show the women why they should yield to him, but concentrated on the much more subtle question 'Why not?' a question very difficult to answer. He was the father of a number of illegitimate children, and I remember my father once saying in a vexed voice, 'Why, the man canna look at a woman, it seems, withoot putting her in the family way!' I was too young at the time to understand these words" (Auto, 17). Other incidents handled in The Three Brothers from a third-person point of view—those of a betrayed woman attacking her seducer, two men fighting in the street, the deaths of David's mother and his brother Sandy, and others—are given in *An Autobiography* as the first-person experiences of Edwin Muir. But were the incidents of the novel entirely fictitious, then the sensitive, personal outlook of David Blackadder, so exactly that of Edwin Muir as it is expressed in *An Autobiography* and other writings, would allow him to be treated as a projection of the novelist's own personality.

Having used autobiographical details in a historical setting, Muir evidently gained the confidence to treat them in their own setting and time in *Poor Tom*, juxtaposing for dramatic effect the actual events of almost a decade into a fictional two-year period. It is true that Muir disclaimed autobiographical sources for the novel,[5] but the evidence of the novel itself outweighs his protestations. Indeed the best chapters are those about events which he describes in *An Autobiography* as his own experiences during his youth and early manhood in Glasgow. Mansie marches with the Clarion Scouts, "enclosed in peace" and "embedded in fold after fold of security." He looks about him and sees a man carrying a little girl on his shoulder:

Mansie could not take his eyes from her, and when the procession began to move, when, in a long line like the powerful and easy rise and fall of a quiet surge, the ranked shoulders in front of him swung up and down, bearing forward on their surface that gay and fragile little bark, unexpected tears rose into Mansie's throat. But when presently from the front of the procession the strains of the "Marseillaise" rolled back towards him over the surface of that quietly rising and falling sea, gathering force as it came until at last it broke round him in a stationary storm of sound in which his own voice was released, he no longer felt that the little girl riding on the shoulder of the surge was more beautiful than anything else, for everything was transfigured. . . . His arms and shoulders sprouted like a tree, scents of spring filled his nostrils, and when, still gazing in a trance at the bareheaded man with the little girl on his shoulder, he also took off his hat, his brows branched and blossomed. . . .[6]

The procession passes through the slums, and Mansie's euphoria influences even his attitude to the jeering crowds along the way. After the procession reaches Glasgow Green, "the spell did not lose its power, and Mansie wandered from platform to platform, where Socialist orators, still transfigured so that he scarcely recognized them, spoke of the consummated joys of the future society where all people would live together in love and joy" (*PT*, 105 - 106).

About 1906 Muir actually joined the Clarion Scouts, a "*do*

something to make the world better" club sponsored by Robert Blatchford's newspaper, the *Clarion*.[7] By the time he was twenty-one he had been converted to Socialism, which gave him "a future in which everything, including [him]self, was transfigured. . . ." When he wrote his autobiography, he remembered that his "sense of human potentiality was so strong that even the lorry-men and the slum boys were transformed by it; I no longer saw them as they were, but as they would be when the society of which I dreamed was realized. . . . For the first time in my life I began to like ordinary vulgar people, because in my eyes they were no longer ordinary or vulgar, since I saw in them shoots of the glory which they would possess when all men and women were free and equal. . . . It was a state which did not last for long; but having once known it I could sometimes summon it back again" (*Auto*, 113).

The detachment of this later evaluation is in fact also present in *Poor Tom*, for the description of the May Day parade continues with Mansie wondering "whether he had talked a great deal of nonsense during the day" and deciding that "everything was allowed." He ends the day in his original "blissful security" (*PT*, 106 - 107), and the bubble of euphoria bursts only in the following chapter: "[A]s his exaltation of the last few days gradually oozed out of him and he returned to a more comfortable size it was actually a relief—he couldn't but admit it to himself, it was an undeniable relief, though it left a sort of empty feeling somewhere. His feet were on the earth again. Strange how easily you slipped back into your old feelings! And when a man turned round to him and asked how he had liked his first procession, he said carelessly, 'Oh, it was quite all right in its way' "(*PT*, 109). Muir's change of style between the two chapters is intentional: the account of the parade is elated and high-flown and reinforces the quality of Mansie's experience, while the style of passages concerning Mansie's everyday life is pedestrian. The high-flown prose reveals Muir's most successful writing, for here, as in the early poems, he is closest to success when closest to bathos.

The Three Brothers and *Poor Tom* may profitably be studied as works embodying actual details taken from the novelist's personal experiences, but the relationship of *The Marionette* to Muir's life is found in the use of themes which appear both in the other novels and in the novelist's own life. The most important link among the three novels is found in the theme of the hero and his brothers. The theme is quite obvious in the two later novels, while in *The Marionette* it is treated in a highly stylized manner. The realization that the three male dolls are Han's "brothers" helps one to understand that Hans is himself as limited as a wooden doll, powerless to act for himself and subject always to stronger wills. He may be taken as a rendition in fiction of Muir's own attitude to his life in earlier years. The sketch Muir gives of himself in the "Fairport" chapter of *An Autobiography* shows the same submissiveness that is exaggerated to a surrealistic level in the character of Hans, whose inarticulateness appears to correspond to Muir's own failure to make any satisfactory response to life for so many years before his marriage.

The reader must view Hans as being on the level of a wooden doll if he is to appreciate the role which the Gretchen marionette plays in the novel. She fills the same part that Ellen (in *The Three Brothers*) and Helen (in *Poor Tom*) play, that of the betraying heroine.[8] Possibly because his characters are so thoroughly disguised Muir employs more violent action in this story than in his other two works. The betrayal in *The Marionette* (which has many overtones depending on the Crucifixion) takes place in the garden of Hans's home when neighborhood boys throw stones across the fence at Hans, and the Gretchen marionette, which is with him, does not "protect" him but remains with the other wooden dolls. The climax of the novel occurs when Hans "murders" Gretchen by repeatedly piercing her body with a nail: the symbolism is perhaps too apparent (*M*, 163 - 66).

This theme of the betraying heroine is also present in the other two novels. The treatment of the theme in *The Three Brothers* is almost as spectacular as that in *The Marionette*. David is actually betrayed by Ellen, who is seduced by his twin brother, Archie, and later murdered by a former fiancé. In *Poor Tom* there is little melodrama in the betrayal of Tom, which is symbolized in Chapter Four when Helen throws the locket Tom gave her into the sea. Mansie feels that Helen's turning to him is in some way the cause of Tom's illness, and he finally gives up Helen to reconcile himself with his brother and to remain constantly by his deathbed. The themes of the hero and his brothers and the betraying heroine are thus related through fraternal rivalry and jealousy, exemplified in the love of the brothers for the same girl.

Other familial relationships in the novels provide themes which can be traced directly to Muir's own life. The death of the hero's mother is in each novel an important influence upon him: Hans's mother dies at his birth, and David's mother, halfway through the novel, while the death of Mansie's mother is predicted in the closing chapters. The father-son relationship is more mechanically formed: either the son is extremely close to his father, as Hans and David are, each being indeed the sole object of his father's love, or the son has no contact at all with the father, as is the case with Mansie.

These fictional themes closely parallel Muir's own life, and these novels may be considered as Muir's attempts to objectify and rid himself of certain fears and other emotions. They especially reveal his relationships with his immediate family. In *The Marionette* and *The Three Brothers* he creates a father-son relationship which is obviously a wish fulfillment based upon his own experiences as the youngest son of an old father. In *Poor Tom* he restricts himself to the actual situation, giving the father no part in the development of Mansie. Likewise, in the same novel his treatment of the mother is based upon the actual truth: Mrs. Manson is a background figure whose presence, if shadowy, influences the characters and events. In his first novel he attempts not to write about the mother-son relationship, perhaps because the death of his mother, an event which haunted him for many years, was too close to him to be externalized, even in the surrealistic disguise which *The Marionette* afforded him. In his second novel he reverses his relationship with his own parents, making David (his proto-self) the favorite of the father and not of the mother, who indeed rejects him in favor of his twin brother. One need not be a Freudian, or even a psychologist, to appreciate this mechanical reversal and use of opposites.

The story of the first novel is at the furthest possible remove from the author, who protects himself from discovery and personal criticism by making the principal figure a half-wit, a type of character through whom any emotion can be expressed. In his second novel, Muir, having achieved a more objective attitude to his life, is able to treat it in an almost direct fashion, interposing only a time difference between his novel and the autobiographical events therein chronicled. Finally in *Poor Tom* he handles his story directly, using both the scene and time of the actual events. Muir's increased objectivity about himself is also seen in his treatment of the heroes in *The Three Brothers* and *Poor Tom*. David Blackadder is an ideal character, a person enjoying relationships such as Muir may have desired for himself, while Mansie Manson is Muir himself, seen in the harshest light possible.

While these themes are more or less directly related to the novelist's own life, they also possess a mythical quality or pattern: the themes are archetypal, significant not merely for Muir alone, but for men in all ages. Of these archetypal themes, the most important is that of the hero's search for an understanding of his life, and indeed, all three novels might well be called *initiation* novels. In *The Marionette* and *The Three Brothers* the father is directly responsible for the son's abortive attempts at understanding himself: Hans, because of his withdrawn condition, can never come to grips with life, and David, because of his innocence, cannot understand the world until he moves farther away from his Eden. The first novel ends somewhat abruptly because Muir realized that Hans, as a fictional character, could never complete the search and hence was of no further value. *The Three Brothers*, however, ends with the search continuing: David wishes to leave his father, and "it was decided that he should try England first, and if he did not like it go over to Holland to his friend Cranstoun" (*TB*, 343). Finally, in *Poor Tom* the hero's search is rewarded, for as Mansie stands by Tom's coffin he is given a vision of the world and his place in it:

Mansie stood without moving, breathed in the scent of the lilies, and no longer felt any desire to go away; for though he knew that he was standing here in the parlour with his dead brother, something so strange had happened that it would have rooted him to a place where he desired far less to be: the walls had receded, the walls of the whole world had receded, and soundlessly a vast and perfect circle—not the provisional circle of life, which can never be fully described—had closed, and he stood within it. He did not know what it was that he divined and bowed down before: everlasting and perfect order, the eternal destiny of all men, the immortality of his own soul; he could not have given utterance to it, although it was so clear and certain; but he had a longing to fall on his knees. . . . [N]othing less than death could erase all wrong and all memory of wrong, leaving the soul free for perfect friendship. . . . [H]e wanted to experience again, like someone learning a lesson, all that he had already experienced; for it seemed a debt due by him to life from which he had turned away, which he had walked round until his new road seemed the natural one, although it had led him to places where all life was frozen to rigidity. . . . He was in haste to begin, and with a last glance at Tom's face, which he could only dimly discern now, for darkness was falling, he left the room and closed the door after him (*PT*, 251 - 54).

Significantly, Edwin Muir wrote no more novels when he had finished *Poor Tom*.

Although these three novels are highly significant in Muir's personal and aesthetic development, they obviously do not bear comparison with the innovative novels of the period, those by James Joyce, Virginia Woolf, and D. H. Lawrence; but they can certainly hold their own with the more usual novels of the period. Like the majority of novelists Muir uses his own life as the material for his fiction.

Yet while most of these novelists, having written about themselves, go on to other themes, Muir, having once successfully delineated his own life, abandoned the novel form. His novels are more than reconstructed diaries, however, for in them Muir is almost always able to derive universal truths from his private experiences; and they could certainly be put forward as models for aspiring novelists who wish to handle their own experiences in fictional modes.

II *The Autobiographies*

Although Muir learned to use autobiographical themes in the medium of prose with only the thinnest of disguises by 1932, he was longer in gaining such skill in poetry; and it is only in *The Narrow Place* (1943) and subsequent collections that one finds the poetic equivalent of *Poor Tom*: a handling of autobiographical themes which is both detached and intimate. This poetic development followed—and indeed may even have been dependent upon—Muir's publishing his autobiography in 1940. James Olney describes autobiography as being "like a magnifying lens, focusing and intensifying that same peculiar creative vitality that informs all the volumes of [the artist's] collected works; it is the symptomatic key to all else that he did and, naturally, to all that he was."[9] In Muir's case there is the further refinement that only after the focusing and intensifying allowed by the direct contemplation of his life could the poet consciously write poems which came from his innermost being and derive visionary knowledge from his personal experiences. Certainly, whatever the absolute reasons for Muir's poetic growth in the late 1930s, in *The Story and the Fable* (1940) and its expansion, *An Autobiography* (1954), Muir shows himself to be what Lord Butler describes as "the ideal apologist pro vita sua" who combines "poetic subjectivity . . . with ruthless objectivity."[10] Kathleen Raine, one of Muir's most able and sympathetic critics, has written that such autobiographies as his, which tell "of experiences in the world of thought and imagination," are "akin to poetry";[11] and indeed *The Story and the Fable* marks the beginning of Muir's emergence as a significant poet. It seems not improbable that his direct examination of his personal yet archetypal experiences which are the source of his mature poems may well have been a cause of his poetic development.

Another fact which influences this development is Muir's religious experience in 1939. He had grown up in a religious home and even experienced several "conversions" as a youth; but during his troubled years in Glasgow he turned away from his childhood faith and for many years had little to do with orthodox Christianity. In the 1930s he became increasingly discontented with his life; and then in 1939 Willa Muir fell dangerously ill. In *An Autobiography* he recalls this time:

I was returning from the nursing home one day—it was the last day of February 1939—when I saw some school-boys playing at marbles on the pavement; the old game had "come round" again at its own time, known only to children, and it seemed a simple little rehearsal for a resurrection, promising a timeless renewal of life. I wrote in my diary next day:

Last night, going to bed alone, I suddenly found myself (I was taking off my waistcoat) reciting the Lord's Prayer in a loud, emphatic voice—a thing I had not done for many years—with deep urgency and profound disturbed emotion. While I went on I grew more composed; as if it had been empty and craving and were being replenished, my soul grew still; every word had a strange fullness of meaning which astonished and delighted me. It was late; I had sat up reading; I was sleepy; but as I stood in the middle of the floor half-undressed, saying the prayer over and over, meaning after meaning sprang from it, overcoming me again with joyful surprise; and I realized that this simple petition was always universal and always inexhaustible, and day by day sanctified human life (*Auto*, 246).

This revelation of religious belief caused no overt change in Muir's life or work; rather it released him from laboring to express any particular belief and allowed him to write more directly from his inner experience without any sort of hindrance. Just as he had to look directly at his own life experiences before he could successfully use them, so he had to acknowledge his innate religious faith before he could successfully assume any religious or philosophical stance.

While *The Story and the Fable* initiates the final, mature period of Edwin Muir's literary career and also provides clues to his artistic development, it is also an outstanding example of the art of autobiography. Richard Hoggart, discussing the problems in this type of writing, speaks of the need to find a "tone or voice . . . which could carry a wide and deep range of attitudes and emotions without being socially self-conscious or derivatively literary." Such a voice is rare; and, Hoggart notes:

Among modern autobiographers I know hardly anyone who has found this tone, this clarity which seems almost like talking to the self, since no one is being wooed. Edwin Muir's autobiography has this quality, and about it one can

properly use phrases like "sensitive integrity." He was a poet and used his
poetic skills here in a disciplined way, not like a man taking time off to doodle;
perhaps also he knew more about himself—after facing his great psychological disturbances—than most of us do; and perhaps his Orcadian upbringing—unliterary and free of the class overtones of most places in
Britain—helped too. At any rate his autobiography is both austere and painfully naked in a way that more obviously "sensitive and intimate"
autobiographies are not. [12]

As Hoggart correctly suggests, the merit of *The Story and the Fable*
comes not least from Muir's clear understanding of his subject:

It is clear [Muir writes] that no autobiography can begin with a man's birth,
that we extend far beyond any boundary line which we can set for ourselves in
the past or the future, and that the life of every man is an endlessly repeated
performance of the life of man. It is clear for the same reason that no
autobiography can confine itself to a conscious life, and that sleep, in which
we pass a third of our existence, is a mode of experience, and our dreams a part
of reality. In themselves our conscious lives may not be particularly interesting. But what we are not and can never be, our fable, seems to me in-
conceivably interesting. I should like to write that fable, but I cannot even live
it; and all I could do if I related the outward course of my life would be to show
how I have deviated from it; though even that is impossible, since I do not
know the fable or anyone who knows it. One or two stages in it I can
recognize: the age of innocence and the Fall and all the dramatic conse-
quences which issue from the Fall. But these lie behind experience, not on its
surface; they are not historical events; they are stages in the fable (*Auto*, 48 -
49).

In Muir's recognition that his personal experiences provide insight
into man's life we see the basis for Kathleen Raine's judgment that
"Edwin Muir is a natural Neoplatonist, though he seldom mentions
philosophy [in his autobiographies]. His *Life* is not only a record of a
particular life, but an attempt to discover what life itself is." [13] His artistic achievement depends, at least in part, upon this recognition, for
while he continues to express his experiences through old stories and
myths, after 1940 he is not afraid to look directly at his life. *The Story
and the Fable* is a valuable autobiography because Muir writes with
an understanding of the human predicament and of his own
relationship to mankind; and because of this new awareness, he is able
to achieve a universality in his imaginative writings.

Ostensibly following the chronology of Muir's life, the structure of
the autobiography actually develops from the theme of earlier

writings: the contrast between order and anarchy, represented as the right and wrong roads which man may follow in life. These "roads" are places which Muir actually knew, the Orkney Islands standing for order, and Glasgow, for anarchy. Even though Muir finally realizes that both order and anarchy are within himself and are not the properties of actual places, his "fable" is inextricably involved with places and, consequently, with time. Because he was born in the remote Orkneys he is one of the few twentieth-century artists with a personal knowledge of a pre-Industrial Age way of life in which (as in the archetypal world he believed it to resemble) time was of little importance and changes rarely came. He declares that he was born in 1737, not because Orkney life was like that of the eighteenth century, but because that date, one hundred and fifty years before his own birth, came before the Industrial Revolution. His childhood was untouched by modernism: "The Orkney I was born into was a place where there was no great distinction between the ordinary and the fabulous; the lives of living men turned into legend" (*Auto*, 14). Daily life had changed little in past centuries, for the Orkney farm was "virtually self-supporting," producing its own food, while sheep provided wool for bankets and cloth (*Auto*, 59). Timelessness manifested itself in the relationships established through the years between men and their neighbors, and between men and the animals which supported them.

Muir's picture of Orkney social life is that of a traditional society in which even the language exemplifies the instinctive social behavior. "The second person singular was in full working order," Muir remembers, "and we used it as it is used in French and German, addressing our friends as 'thu' and 'thee' and strangers and official personages as 'you'; we had a sure sense of the distinction and were never at a loss" (*Auto*, 62). Orkney life remained always for Muir an example of order. "I cannot say how much my idea of a good life was influenced by my early upbringing," he writes, "but it seems to me that the life of the little island of Wyre was a good one, and that its sins were mere sins of the flesh, which are excusable, and not sins of the spirit" (*Auto*, 63). This traditional life also brought about the relationships Muir discerns between men and their animals: "My passion for animals," he writes, "comes partly from being brought up so close to them, in a place where people lived as they had lived for two hundred years; partly from I do not know where. Two hundred years ago the majority of people lived close to the animals by whose labour or flesh they existed. The fact that we live on these animals remains; but the personal relation is gone, and with it the very ideas of necessity

and guilt. The animals we eat are killed by thousands in slaughter-
houses which we never see. A rationalist would smile at the thought
that there is any guilt at all: there is only necessity, he would say, a
necessity which is laid upon all carnivores, not on man only. But our
dreams and ancestral memories speak a different language . . ."
(*Auto*, 48). Here, without the equivocation found in earlier writings,
Muir accepts "dreams and ancestral memories" as final authorities.

The accuracy and truth of these memories of the Orkneys do not
matter: Muir believes that he experienced a living example of an
archetypal society, a "good order" whose pattern evolved in man's
collective, unconscious life and in which there was no conflict
between the conscious self and the unconscious. For his first fourteen
years Edwin knew a way of life which, in spite of its drawbacks and
deprivations, was essentially whole: it had a center and things did not
fall apart.

In 1901 the Muir family left the Orkney Islands and moved to
Glasgow. "When I arrived," Muir writes, "I found that it was not
1751, but 1901, and that a hundred and fifty years had been burned
up in two days' journey. But I myself was still in 1751, and remained
there for a long time. All my life since I have been trying to overhaul
that invisible leeway. No wonder I am obsessed with
Time."[14] The central part of *The Story and the Fable* concerning
Edwin's years in Glasgow tells mainly the "story" of his life: the
"fable" was lost to him, and later he sees these years as "a long illness" from which he had recovered and as the manifestations of the
anarchy which obscured his archetypal path. He escaped this existence only through his marriage: "If my wife had not encouraged
me," he acknowledges, "it is unlikely that I should have taken the
plunge [to leave Glasgow] myself; I was still paralysed by my inward
conflict"(*Auto*, 154).

In the last part of *the Story and the Fable* Muir describes his life in
London and on the Continent between 1919 and 1922. His marriage,
his analysis, and time (and perhaps distance) aided in bringing
together his long-separated "story" and "fable."

I reached a state which resembled conviction of sin, though formulated in
different terms. I realized the elementary fact that every one, like myself, was
troubled by sensual desires and thoughts, by unacknowledged failures and
frustrations causing self-hatred and hatred of others, by dead memories of
shame and grief which had been shovelled underground long since because
they could not be borne. I saw that my lot was the human lot, that when I
faced my own unvarnished likeness I was one among all men and women, all

of whom had the same desires and thoughts, the same failures and frustrations, the same unacknowledged hatred of themselves and others, the same hidden shames and griefs, and that if they confronted these things they could win a certain liberation from them. It was really a conviction of sin, but even more a realization of Original Sin. It took a long time to crystallize. It was not a welcome realization, for nothing is harder than to look at yourself. . . . It was not till . . . we were staying in Prague, that I knew how much good the analyst had done me: my vague fears, I realized one day, were quite gone (*Auto*, 158 - 59).

This "recovery" was greatly aided by the several years of comparative idleness which the Muirs had in Europe: a period which he afterwards called "my turning point . . . when my past life came alive in me after lying for so long, dead weight, my actual life came alive too as that new life passed into it; for it was new, though old; indeed, I felt that only now was I truly living it, since only now did I see it as it was, so that at last it could become experience. Without those few years of idleness, of looking and looking back, I might never have really lived my life. I was thirty-five then, and passing through a stage which, if things had been different, I should have reached ten years earlier. I have felt that handicap ever since. I began to write poetry at thirty-five instead of at twenty-five or twenty."[15]

The Story and the Fable ends with Muir's beginning his professional career as a writer, the beginning, one might say, of his "story." His aim had been to recreate the "fable" of his life, and the excellence of his work is due to his accomplishing this goal. Indeed, his success in the 1940 autobiography causes some of the differences between it and the 1954 revision, for, having entered into a more active, worldly life, in the later work he inevitably stresses his "story," even revising the earlier section to the extent that the intimate, personal tone is often diminished.

The differences between the two books also reflect the change in Muir's life after he began working for the British Council. In 1940 introspective contemplation governed his life and thought, whereas in 1954 he had participated for well over a decade in the world of activity. Caught up in daily affairs he remembers mainly the outline of past events, rather than their details, his dulled memory being most obvious in Chapters Seven, Eight, and Nine, the continuation of his life story in the 1920s. The last chapter of *The Story and the Fable*, centered on his awakening to his new life, is even more vivid when it is followed in *An Autobiography* by this recital of his and Willa's visit to Salzburg:

In that lovely provincial town we became acquainted with a thing which was to cause the extermination of five million people twenty years later. In a *café* we came across a little local paper called *Der Eiserne Besen*, the Iron Broom. It contained nothing but libellous charges against local Jews, set down with great rancour. . . . And in a bookshop where I went one day to buy the poems of Walther von der Vogelweide, the proprietor, who was embarrassingly grateful for my interest in German poetry, became rude when I asked him for the poems of Hugo von Hofmannsthal; he said roughly that he did not stock them. I could not understand his sudden incivility, and only after I had left did I begin to realize that he must have thought it presumptuous for any Jew, or anyone partly Jewish, like Hofmannsthal, to write in German (*Auto*, 214 - 15).

Muir no longer focuses on his personal response, but on his place in the context of social events. He is not unaware of his changed point of view, for he writes, in the paragraph immediately following, that "my wife and I were our own chief company, and perfectly content to be so. We shared a common experience whose double reflection, thrown from one to the other, composed itself into a single image. That was our greatest pleasure. Yet, in the thirty years since, these impressions, which gave us so much pleasure then, have faded, and when I try to resurrect them now everything becomes insubstantial" (*Auto*, 215).

The later-written parts of *An Autobiography* are narrative rather than contemplative; and the different point of view makes possible a quiet humor in certain passages, as in Muir's recollection of the house he rented in Hampstead in the 1930s:

[It was] an old dilapidated Strawberry Hill Gothic house, which vibrated gently whenever the underground train passed beneath it. A plumber and repairer had attended to it for an absentminded trust for forty years. Plumbing had developed during that time, but he had not. The roof of our bedroom leaked, and for the first few weeks we had to sleep with a large umbrella over our heads, in case of rain. We got him to put in a new bath, but he absentmindedly left the waste-pipe hanging in the air, and the first time the bath was filled water poured down into the dining-room below, bringing a large chunk of plaster with it. The lavatory pan swayed precariously when you sat on it (*Auto*, 237).

In *An Autobiography* the peculiarities and eccentricities of the poet's "story" take precedence over his "fable," which appears only in isolated recollections; Muir is no longer concerned solely with himself, but also with his relationship to society. When he writes of events closer to 1954 there is the further difference that he expresses himself in a more self-conscious way. He describes his visit to Nuremberg in 1945: he and his companions "clambered over the ruins of the old town," and, Muir writes, "I remembered a few days I had spent there with my wife during our stay in Hellerau. The town had enchanted us; so much affection had gone into the building of it; every house was a simple embodiment of the impulse which makes people create a little world around them to which they can attach their affections. Now nothing was left but jagged blocks of masonry. As I clambered over the debris I tried to find Dürer's house and the little fountain in the square, but nothing seemed to be left except some fragments of the city wall" (*Auto*, 254). This recital of facts is so arranged that the way in which the sentences are pivoted on the simple statement in the center, "Now nothing was left but jagged blocks of masonry," conveys those emotions not described. In *An Autobiography* "the glory and the dream" are dimmed, but they are replaced by a calm reflection which is as attractive as the excited immediacy of *The Story and the Fable*. Muir's revisions do not cause the initial inspiration to be lost, and thus *An Autobiography* presents two equally faithful delineations of its writer. The picture is that of a circle growing ever larger, the author at the center being aware first of only his own feelings and ideas, but moving then toward the perimeter of man in all his relationships—to nature, to society, and to God.

CHAPTER 5

The Poet: Poems of the 1920s and Early 1930s

A LTHOUGH Edwin Muir stands apart from the experimental poets whose innovations have changed the course of twentieth-century literature, he holds an important place in the tradition of contemplative verse. His poems reflect not his age but rather traditional wisdom seen through his age, while his philosophy, although influenced by the movements of his time, is basically neo-Platonic and Christian. The nature of his poems can perhaps best be understood by remembering that he was thirty-five years old when he seriously began writing verse, and that he was well into his fifties before he consistently expressed himself with skill and created poems of lasting value. Because of his maturity—and also because of his position as an established writer—his first verses express many of the same ideas and themes that are found in his last poems. The turning point in Muir's poetic development came in the late 1930s and was associated with the writing of his autobiography and his acknowledgment of his Christian faith. Thus the poems that he wrote before this time can be considered together, the only differences in them being the developing technical facility. [1]

I First Poems *(1925) and* Chorus of the Newly Dead *(1926)*

In his first book of verse Muir arranged the poems so that they either repeat or contrast the ideas of succeeding poems and thus create an overall meaning for the collection. The general theme has to do with time: poems concerning time past, the "lost"time of childhood, are followed by those concerning time present, a meaningless or illusionary entity—one of these poems is appropriately entitled "Maya" (*FP*, 19). The poet considers man's despair in "An Ancient Song" and the conflict of time and beauty in "Betrayal"; and he finds a resolution for this conflict in "Anatomy," deciding that "Toward changelessness my members change" (*FP*, 29, 30, 32). He approaches even closer to a point of stasis in "Logos," when he realizes that man has divine origins and is a traveler on an "immense eternal pathway" (*FP*, 33). Finally, in the last three autumnal poems, he is content to accept the sleeping earth and its beauty. In addition to the eighteen poems, *First Poems* also includes six ballads, three of them based upon dreams that Muir transcribed in prose in *An Autobiography;* the other three ballads are retellings of old stories and myths. The "Ballad of the Flood" is one of Muir's few attempts to write in Scots (*CP*, 31). Years later the poet called this ballad "the most Scottish poem I ever wrote." It, like all of his ballads, has the authentic ballad feel; but only the "Ballad of Hector in Hades" comes up to the level of the prose version of the same material (*CP*, 24). In it (the "best . . . in the book," in the judgment of Peter Butter)[2] Muir remembers how he ran away from a childhood fight with another boy, seeing the experience as that of Hector in Hades, who must eternally run from the pursuing Achilles. The excellence of the poem comes from the congruence of theme and expression, an inevitability which is often lacking in the other poems.

When Louis Untermeyer reviewed the *First Poems*, he remarked that "one looks—and looks in vain—for that mixture of audacious gaiety and volative illumination which makes Muir's essays so brilliant and distinctive."[3] Certainly these poems are at a considerable distance from the essays and reviews. The clue to their enigmatic vitality lies in seeing them in terms of what, for convenience, may be called Jungian psychology. Muir realized the psychological origins of his verses, writing of the "Ballad of Rebirth" (*FP*, 48) that "it was not 'I' who dreamt it, but something else which the psychologists call the racial unconscious, and for which there are other names."[4] Muir was one of those rare individuals who possess an intuitive awareness of archetypes; and during and after his analysis, he often stressed in his essays the necessity of "individuation," the Jungian idea of "activat[ing] the forces of the unconscious and . . . integrat[ing] these contents into the psychic totality."[5] He only gradually became aware that his poetry came from such a source and did not in fact learn to control that source until the early 1940s. Muir's friend John Holms, having read these first poems in manuscript, once wrote with calculated exaggeration to Hugh Kingsmill, " 'If [Muir] hasn't a dream to inspire him, his verses are commonplace.' "[6]

Yet technique, rather than inspiration, causes the most problems,

for more than any other poet of his stature, Muir labored long to find
the appropriate expression for his poetic vision. He never doubted his
vision and declared later that he began "to write poetry simply
because what I wanted to say could not have gone properly into prose.
I wanted so much to say it that I had no thought left to study the form
in which alone it could be said."[7] These early poems reflect an uneasy
balance of content and expression, for while some are the direct expression of an unwilled archetypal vision, others, drawn from the
same source, have been consciously shaped by the poet. Such directly
archetypal poems as the "Ballad of Rebirth" and "Ballad of Eternal
Life" (later renamed "Ballad of the Soul" [*CP*, 26]) are intensely personal and private; and only such controlled poems as "Logos" allow
meaningful insights. "Logos" is a vision poem in which the speaker
moves back through time and space to the silence of the eternity in
which the earth was created: "The hills are eaten / Away in silence."

> End and Beginning!
> Thy tides are warm and stagnant.
> In caverns, snow-white giants
> Sprawl on great rocks, and the currents
> Lift and let fall their foam-soft crumbling
> Limbs, and their eyes more clear than water
> Laugh when the waves comb out their tresses.
> Their hands are vague and careless
> As lazy tree-tops swaying.
> On their huge breasts hang generations
> Asleep, like sunless forests.
> Light shall bear these, whom darkness ripened.
> They shall know naught save that in slumber
> Mysterious fingers
> Touched them, and their blood yearned upward
> Chafing against sealed ears and eyelids.
>   (*FP*, 33 - 34)

Muir acknowledges here man's spiritual origin in this union of the
"Logos" and the "generations asleep," an act which takes place under water. The primary image is that of a divine generation and is the
same image which stands behind the story of Danäe, behind the concept of the Holy Grail (according to Jessie Weston), and behind the
myth of Leda and the Swan, to mention only three instances treated
by poets in the past hundred years. But unlike Tennyson, Eliot, and
Yeats, Muir goes directly to the archetype, for "Logos" is the antithesis of the poetry of allusion: it is direct statement.

This quality of direct statement has much to do with the artistry of "Horses," in which Muir watches the plow-horses "on the bare field" and remembers how as a child he saw

> Their hooves like pistons in an ancient mill
> Move up and down, yet seem as standing still.
>
> Their conquering hooves which trod the stubble down
> Were ritual that turned the field to brown,
> And their great hulks were seraphim of gold,
> Or mute ecstatic monsters on the mould.
>
> . . . .
>
> But when at dusk with steaming nostrils home
> They came, they seemed gigantic in the gloam,
> And warm and glowing with mysterious fire
> That lit their smouldering bodies in the mire.
>   (*CP*, 20)

The poem is disarmingly simple, yet, as Ralph Mills writes, in it Muir creates "the atmosphere and dimension of a primordial myth."[8] There is a similar level of achievement in those other poems in which Muir is able directly to state his personal experience—"Childhood," for example, and "Autumn in Prague" and "October at Hellbrünn" (*CP*, 19, 23)—but too often, however, the medium of the verse comes between him and his idea, and difficulties of diction, of form, and of meter cause the personal vision to be obscured or lost.

This problem causes the failure of the *Chorus of the Newly Dead*. This poem consists of seven monologues by different speakers, introduced, linked together, and concluded by choruses. The speakers—the Idiot, the Beggar, the Coward, the Harlot, the Poet, the Hero, and the Mystic—are "the dead . . . [who] look back at the life they had left and contemplate it from their new station." Muir was immensely excited by the poem and worked on it for several years.[9] In a letter to Sydney Schiff he describes his aims: the characters, he writes, "will all give some account of their lives as they see it from eternity, not in Heaven or in Hell, but in a dubious place where the bewilderment of the change has not been lost. There will also be choruses for all the newly dead in which some kind of transcendental judgment will be passed on these recitals as they arise. . . . I hope that in the end a feeling of gratification will be given by the poem as a whole."[10] After the Woolfs published the

poem, Muir rewrote various verses, but he finally realized that his
"imaginative excitement never managed to communicate itself, or at
best now or then, to the poem."[11] Peter Butter has written at length
about the *Chorus*, calling it "a brave attempt to deal with a large
theme; it contains some impressive visions and some lovely lines and
stanzas, and deserves reprinting. It was a very original poem to have
written in the early 1920s."[12]

On the whole, however, most of the language and stanza forms
detract from the meaning. The technical limitations are even more
obvious when one realizes that many of the images and concepts also
appear in later, more fluent poems. The last five stanzas of "The
Mystic" illustrate this point:

> But oh, that clear angelic host
>   Of mountains standing in the sky!
> That dragon-wrought long silent coast
>   Where wheeling sun and stars went by!
>
> Those proud heraldic animals
>   Like pictures in a primal dream,
> Holding unconscious festivals
>   Which past our primal darkness gleam!
>
> That stationary country where
>   Achilles drives and Hector runs,
> Making a movement in the air
>   Forever, under all the suns!
>
> And that ghostly eternity
>   Cut by the bridge where journeys Christ,
> On endless arcs pacing the sea,
>   Time turning with his solar tryst!
>
> They sink behind me. Fate is here,
>   Approaching, stumbling through the deep.
> And once again the primal fear
>   Falls, and I wake from sleep to sleep.
>   (*CND*, 15)

The single images which make up the static vision are expressed in
memorable language, but almost without exception the quatrains
break in half, for, apart from the rhyme, there is no necessary
relationship between the two halves. And when Muir attempts to integrate these separate pictures into the dramatic framework of the

poem, the diction, the relentless rhyme, and the confusion as to the identity of the speaker spoil the effect. Yet here are also the images and even phrases which, unchanged in later poems, evoke the reader's unqualified praise. The limitations are not merely of technique; they have to do rather with the nature of the poet's inspiration. The *Chorus of the Newly Dead* is willed verse, originating in intellectual processes rather than intuitive responses and therefore alien to Edwin Muir's native genius. Although there are archetypal images in the poem, the majority derive from a finite, caused symbolism in which each symbol leads the reader back to one thought or to one act, and no further. They are not entrances into a whole way of thinking about man—as some of the *First Poems* are—but barricades erected by each individual in the poem around himself. The *Chorus* was an ambitious project, but not a successful one; and the decision not to reprint it shows Muir's mature artistic judgment.

II   Six Poems *(1932)*

Muir's uncertainty as to what his true poetic expression should be also influences *Six Poems*.[13] Again the poems are written within the forms of traditional verse; and again at least two of them, "The Stationary Journey" and "Transmutation," deal with time and man's subjection to it (*CP*, 57, 85). But in "The Stationary Journey" Muir begins to develop the voice he continues to use in later poems: it is that of a sort of Everyman who has lived through all time and who, being the inheritor of all men's development, wonders in this poem whether, if he could "Retrace the path that led [him] here," he could "find a different way." He moves backward through time to reach an archetypal world from which all being originates and in which all things and events are coexistent. But the speaker is unable to find a resolution of his vision, and the poem comes to an abrupt conclusion:

> A dream! the astronomic years
>   Patrolled by stars and planets bring
> Time led in chains from post to post
>   Of the all-conquering Zodiac ring.
>   (*CP*, 59)

Although the poem as a whole lacks the affirmative belief which characterizes the mature verse, this last stanza shows Muir's ability to fuse within the narrowest limits images with such disparate origins as history, medieval science, and metaphysics, while also sounding the tone that is frequently heard in his later verse.

The other poems reveal a tendency which actually grew upon Muir and for which he was often criticized, even in his last years, the device of using old stories as vehicles for his ideas. In *Six Poems* the practice manifests itself in the subjects: "The Trance" retells Keats's "La Belle Dame Sans Merci," while "Tristram Crazed" treats the legend of Tristram and Iseult (*CP*, 74, 64), and "The Field of the Potter," the story of Judas's betrayal of Christ (*SP*, 7). In later years Muir even echoes the words or cadences of other poets. Sometimes he does so for a deliberate contrast between his ideas and those of the poet he imitates, but not infrequently the "echoes" are quite unconscious. Perhaps, in view of his wide reading for his reviews, essays, and books, it is not surprising that many of his poems have this "bookish" or literary flavor. "Tristram Crazed" expresses ideas he was considering in his contemporary essays, such as, for example, that of recurrence: Tristram journeys away from Tintagel:

> And hill and plain and wood and tower
> Passed on and on and turning came
> Back to him, tower and wood and hill,
> Now different, now the same.

And like Hans, Muir's protofigure in *The Marionette*, Tristram cannot distinguish illusion from reality:

> There was a castle on a lake.
> The castle doubled in the mere
> Confused him, his uncertain eye
> Wavered from there to here.
>
> (*CP*, 64)

The last of these *Six Poems* is "The Fall," another archetypal poem in which the speaker asks, "What was I ere I came to man?" and ponders over the "shapes" he may have seen "that once / Agelong through endless Eden ran." Perhaps among them were "the dragon brood" from whose "amber eyeballs fell / Soft-rayed the rustling gold." But now, outside Eden, there are no such immortal shapes, for, since "the Fall," there has been only one figure equal to the archetypes of Eden, Christ the Redeemer. But Muir, being unwilling directly to state this idea, consciously obscures it in the last stanzas of the poem by referring to Christ as "the Sphinx" and by likening Him to a "wooden prow" that sails through time and space and

> Whose salt-white brow like crusted fire
> Smiles ever, whose cheeks are red as blood,
> Whose dolphin back is flowered yet
> With wrack that swam upon the Flood.
>
> (*CP*, 68 - 70)

While the speaker makes his own "heaven and Hell / To buy [his] bartered Paradise," he can "see a shadowy figure fall, / And not far off another beats / With his bare hands on Eden's wall" (*CP*, 70). The speaker's struggle is that of all men, repeated through all time.

This use of well-known legends as vehicles contrasts with the contemporary practice of Eliot and other poets who attempt to give additional depth and texture to their verse through literary allusions, since Muir employs such references not for their initial meaning but rather for their value as frameworks for the ideas that preoccupy him and as archetypal stories in their own right. This practice proved increasingly successful, and in later years Muir made extensive use of established stories and legends, investing them with his own original meanings. It may also be significant that Muir wrote these poems while he was retelling his personal experiences in his novels. Expressing himself so fully in his fiction, he obviously felt no need to write very many poems and none on the overtly autobiographical level.

III   Variations on a Time Theme *(1934)*

After Muir stopped writing prose fiction in 1932, he composed more and more poems, publishing fifty or so by 1939. Many of them are difficult to understand, for in these years he was struggling to find a satisfactory attitude to life, and his doubts and confusions frequently make his verse obscure. The *Variations on a Time Theme* consists of ten numbered poems; they appear to form a true theme-with-variations, although seven were separately published with individual titles, and only three were written for the volume. The epigraph—"And another king shall rise after them . . . and think that he may change times and laws, and they shall be given into his hands, until a time, and times, and dividing of times"—is from the book of Daniel (7:24, 25); it is a vision of the passing away of earthly kingdoms and judgments and of the eternal, never-failing rule of Jehovah. It relates to the poems because they show man at the mercy of time. He cannot escape it in the present, and he bears with him all its workings in the past. Although time present has gone wrong for man, the poet does not despair, but rather trusts in man's future escape from time.

The first variation, originally entitled "Interregnum,"[14] develops through rhetorical questions, a device that allows Muir to build up a positive picture by negative means and to suggest rather than declare (CP, 39). Here he states only three things positively: the unpleasantness of the present time; the good which was to be found along the way to this time or place; and the fact that other men will come to the same time. Everything else is cast in the form of a question, as if he were refusing to involve himself with it. The echoes of T. S. Eliot in this poem are so obvious that Muir probably intended them to remind readers of Eliot's poems and thus to function like the suggestive questions, for by referring to such poems as The Waste Land and The Hollow Men, Muir evokes the appropriate sense of disillusionment and, not establishing it in his poem, concentrates on man's possibilities rather than on his failures in this place and in this time.

Although there are such similarities to Eliot's work, these poems are distinguished by Muir's sanguine faith in man's power to find his way out of his predicament. A literary parallel for Muir's attitude may be found in Kafka's stories, or, rather, in Muir's concept of Kafka's thought. Both writers believe that a road leads through life which man must follow, that this road has not only a beginning but an ending, and that a Deity governs man's activities. They differ in their attitude to this God, for Kafka believes that He can be known, while Muir is so aware of man's separation from Him and is so desperate to reconcile man and God that he cannot pause to consider the possibility of knowing God. In spite of his religious preoccupation, Muir expresses his attempt at reconciliation in psychological, not religious, terms.

Thus the second poem (CP, 40 - 42) is a soliloquy spoken by the soul which, thought of as a rider, speaks to the body, the horse, saying that these "horses pace and pace / Like steeds for ever labouring on a shield, / Keeping their solitary heraldic courses," although the riders in turn "fall here on the plain," so that the body never knows the soul which inhabits it, or remembers the "glimmer of autumn life / . . . when our limbs were weightless / As red leaves on a tree, and our silvery breaths / Went on before us like new-risen souls." The speaker has heard that "these beasts are mortal" and that the riders are, "it is said, immortal."

. . . . . . Yet these worn saddles
Have powers to charm us to obliviousness.
They were appointed for us, and the scent of the ancient leather
Is strong as a spell. So we must mourn or rejoice
For this our station, our inheritance
As if it were all. This plain all. This journey all.

(*CP*, 42)

In the fifth variation Muir recognizes the inescapable inheritance of the racial unconscious and uses it to explain his paradoxical idea that all time exists in one time: because of the memories that descend to man, generation after generation, no time is ever lost, for wherever and whenever man lives, time past lives in his unconscious. This fearful inheritance causes Muir to see men's lives as a "Slow-motion flight over a bottomless road," for there is no solid footing when men are at the mercy of such an inheritance. He suggests that the complications of man's progress may be merely a "clinical fantasy begotten by / The knife of demon Time the vivisector / Incising nightmares," but fear outweighs such rationalizations when he looks about him and realizes that the remains of past life are either "Human or bestial—indistinguishable," and that man's face is no more than a "shallow mask" concealing inherited qualities from which he cannot escape. In resignation he concludes, "We have known / Only this debris not yet overgrown, / Never to be removed. / Dead and our own" (*CP*, 44 - 45).

While the images and references in the second variation have a characteristic medieval-heraldic suggestiveness, on the whole the imagery of the *Variations* is eclectic: some images derive from contemporary poetry, others from the tradition of Vaughan and Wordsworth, and still others from the Old Testament. The biblical stories of the Jews provide the framework for several of these poems. In the third variation Muir tells his personal story in terms of Jewish history. Again he speaks for all men who have fallen from Grace, been expelled from Paradise, and must search "for the promised land"; and, as is usually the case when he finds an appropriate vehicle for his thought—in this case, images from the Old Testament—the poem is direct in statement. Yet its conclusion is enigmatic, for the poet does not know how to regard his expulsion from Eden:

As he who snatches all at last will crave
To be of all there is the quivering slave,

So I from base to base slipped headlong down
Till all that glory was my mountainous crown.
Set free, or outlawed, now I walk the sand
And search this rubble for the promised land.
                                        (*CP*, 43)

In the seventh variation Muir expresses man's absolute subjection to time and emphasizes that if there is no "Rescuer" of man from his bondage, then "Imprisonment's for ever; we're the mock of Time, / While lost and empty lies Eternity" (*CP*, 48). Similar concepts are expressed in the following poem, while in the ninth variation the speaker looks more closely at the individual and acknowledges that although Time lies outside him and is unaffected by him, he can control its effect—or he could, were it not that "Packed in my skin from head to toe / Is one I know and do not know. / . . . / His name's Indifference." This alter ego constantly defies "my soul, my Visitor," who could return the poet to the time when "the one Tree/Would stand for ever safe and fair/And Adam's hand stop in the air" (*CP*, 50 - 51). J. R. Watson, in his explication of this poem, notes that "the Soul's foundation is in pity, and this is why it fights indifference. Pity is essential for the conquering of indifference, and this is Muir's answer in this poem to the problem of evil: pity would gladly abolish evil from the earth, but if it did, indifference would reign supreme."[15] The "Soul" is always kept from its goal by "Indifference," and so side by side with the ameliorating power lies the inability to use it. Appropriately the poem was entitled "The Dilemma" when it was first published.

Variations on a Time Theme concludes with a poem in which Muir draws away from the unsolvable problems of time to contemplate the constellations that man recognized and named in past ages and to see the sky as a stationary flag or shield upon which heraldic figures move. He speculates that these creatures—the lion, the dragon—were thrown into the sky by some "fabulous wave far back in Time" so that they cannot recognize "this new world."

Here now heraldic watch them ride
This path far up the mountain-side
And backward never cast a look;
Ignorant that the dragon died
Long since and that the mountain shook
When the great lion was crucified.
                                        (*CP*, 53)

Muir's images rarely have a point-for-point symbolic value, and hence one can only tentatively identify the dragon as primeval man in his first state of innocence and the lion as Christ, but such an equation would agree with the aloofness of the external world, unaware of man's fall from Grace and Christ's sacrifice.

The unity of these poems arises from the common fund of ideas and the similar voice of the speaker, who is generally the poet himself in the role of Everyman. *Variations on a Time Theme* possesses a logical structure and a relationship between form and thought which are lacking in the *Chorus of the Newly Dead*, in spite of the superficial resemblances of the two collections. In the successful poems of the later volume meters and forms work together to produce a quiet, restrained, and even elegiac tone. Muir's most memorable verses present images drawn either from history ("steeds for ever labouring on a shield, / Keeping their solitary heraldic courses") or from the Hebraic-Christian culture in which he was raised ("A child in Adam's field I dreamed away / My one eternity and hourless day, / Ere from my wrist Time's bird had learned to fly") (*CP*, 40, 42); yet, apart from the not-infrequent obscurity, there is the constant threat of weak diction which either through difficult sounds or incongruity with the surrounding words may wreck the poem. The content of the poems is actually religious in nature, although the expression is generally in psychological terms or in psychological situations. The *Variations* and the poems in *Journeys and Places* reflect Muir's personal quandary in these years when he attempted to make out of his psychological studies and rehashed Nietzschean philosophy a substitute for what was ultimately to prove his true orientation to life, a religious point of view.

IV   Journeys and Places *(1937)*

While this "false direction" prevented Muir from reaching his mature religious position and these poems from expressing his most characteristic ideas, it accounts for some of the best qualities in the *Journeys and Places* poems, specifically for Muir's clear expression of archetypal images, as well as for the continued use of the Everyman persona. This Nietzschean figure is caught in an eternal recurrence from which he cannot escape and in which he cannot forget. He remembers all past events and is aware of his dual nature: that he possesses both an ideal self and a real, or at least present, self. Hence the speaker of "The Unfamiliar Place" seeks illumination for the present day; to this end he has "questioned many a ghost," and

Far inland in my dreams,
Enquired of fears and shames
The dark and winding way
To the day within my day.
(*CP*, 78)

Muir clearly states his belief that life is lived over and over in "The Solitary Place," in which the repeated phrase "I and not I" stands for the individual's concept of himself in the present and for his spirit as it goes through the cycles of life and death unchanged. Thus "I and not I" have witnessed "The Cross and the Flood / And Babel's towers / And Abel's blood / And Eden's bowers." The individual's plight in this progression of life is likened to that of

A lost player upon a hill
On a sad evening when the world is still,
The house empty, a brother and sister gone
Beyond the reach of sight, or sound of any cry,
Into the bastion of the mind, behind the shutter of the eye.
(*CP*, 81)

The despair in this poem is unusual for Muir, and indeed the poem had originally an extra stanza—when the *London Mercury* published it as "I and Not I"—in which the poet suggests that "if there is another light . . . And a breath within the light," as well as "a hand [that] comes towards me / To lead me out of me," then he is "not sole, secure, forsaken."[16]

The theme of the individual's duality also appears in "The Private Place," where Muir thinks of himself as held by "This stranger . . . / This deaf usurper I shall never know," who is untroubled by the poet's troubles, "And while I rage is insolent as the dead, / Composed, indifferent, thankless, faithful" (*CP*, 82). In the *Variations* the "stranger" is named "Indifference"; but whatever the name, the duality is that of the conscious and unconscious selves of the individual, for while Muir knows that they always oppose one another, he also realizes that a temporary truce comes from acknowledging the archetypal world which lies behind all life. The all-knowing and all-powerful archetypal figure of man can rescue temporal man from his troubles. Muir also expresses this duality of self in the image of the road through life from which man has strayed. This spatial image allows Muir to think of time past as the place where his road originated. There man can communicate with himself: it is his Eden, for there time is forever static; and the undying sense of loss which man in every generation feels is his regret for this place.

The penultimate poem of *Journeys and Places*, "The Sufficient Place," maps out the world of archetypal images, a place where "all the silver roads wind in." Here is a "little house," a "great hill worn down to a patient mound," and "tall trees" with thick leaves and birds on their branches. In the doorway of the house are

> Two figures, Man and Woman, simple and clear
> As a child's first images. Their manners are
> Such as were known before the earliest fashion
> Taught the Heavens guile. . . . .
> . . . .
> . . . . Here all's sufficient. None
> That comes complains, and all the world comes here,
> Comes, and goes out again, and comes again.
> This is the Pattern, these the Archetypes,
> Sufficient, strong, and peaceful.
>
> (*CP*, 86 - 87)

Muir equates the archetypal world to Eden, an eternal world of peace; and thus the expulsion from the Garden becomes Muir's symbol for modern man's inability to communicate with himself and for his straying from the path through life. In addition to these biblical images (which do not imply a specific religious belief, but are rather the most valid of contemporary cultural symbols for this archetypal situation), Muir also uses the image of the biblical tree of life or, in terms of Scandinavian mythology, the tree of Yggdrasill which binds heaven, earth, and hell together. This "single tree," whose roots are in the underworld and whose branches are in the heavens, represents both order and its archetypal pattern: it is a basic symbol of Muir's poetry in this period.[17]

Muir's concern with time makes it an important theme in its own right. Because man's attempt to find his second self (or road) is pitted against time and its forces, the poet longs for a place in which he possesses all time, one in which the past, the present, and future coexist. Thus, in the highly controlled lyric "The Mountains," although Muir desires to leap "time's bound" (either forward or backward), he must acknowledge that he is tied to the present, where he is forced to watch time's slow progress through the seasons and to dream

> . . . of a peak whose height
> Will show me every hill,
> A single mountain on whose side
> Life blooms for ever and is still.
>   (*CP*, 59 - 60)

There are similar ideas in "The Road," a difficult poem (the "road" of this poem lies in the fourth dimension beyond time and space, turning and twisting in one place), in which Muir again combines Nietzsche's idea of eternal recurrence and the idea that all things are coexistent in order to destroy mechanical time and, consequently, physical space (*CP*, 61 - 62).

While these ideas about time are obviously derived from various Nietzschean concepts, they are also based upon Muir's understanding of archetypes: if a perfect pattern of life exists, so he seems to have reasoned, then all things are implied by it and thus all life coexists eternally. Man's inner life—his phantoms, or ghosts, or racial memories—provides the evidence of such life; and these never-forgotten memories remain a source of knowledge for the individual. It follows then that since the archetypal pattern preordains all life, free will is a delusion and fate rules. Thus the circle is complete; for although Muir formed these ideas after his study of psychology, of Nietzsche, and of philosophy, they repeat his youthful, Calvinistic beliefs in predestination and election. Yet Muir, because of his psychological studies and consequent reorientation to life, was able to transform what he knew initially as negative and foreboding into an optimistic belief, rarely doubting that man would find that road which would lead him to rest and peace. This final stage of his belief can be seen in *Journeys and Places,* particularly in the last poem, "The Dreamt-of Place," a vision-poem in which Muir describes the disappearance of hell and its tortures: the dead look down from Heaven, the living look up from the earth; and "Grass grows upon the surly sides of Hell." This is "the reconciliation, / This is the day after the Last Day" when "Time has caught time and holds it fast forever."

> And then I thought, Where is the knife, the butcher,
> The victim? Are they all here in their places?
> Hid in this harmony? But there was no answer.
>   (*CP*, 88)

Such faith in future good stands behind most of the poems in *Journeys and Places.*

Just as Muir continues to use and to develop these characteristic themes and images, so he continues his practice of writing poems that are based on works of literature, or at least on images from such works. I have already pointed to the Nietzschean and biblical phrases and images; in "The Dreamt-of Place" the *Inferno* supplies the images; and quite often one feels the presence of T. S. Eliot and W. B. Yeats immediately behind the language of various poems. Typically, in "Hölderlin's Journey" Muir takes the historical fact of Hölderlin's mysterious trip from Bordeaux to his "Diotima" in Frankfurt and treats the journey, its doubtful destination, and Hölderlin's questioning of reality as a ready-made vehicle for his own personal ideas. "Diotima" (in reality Susette Gontard) becomes the symbol both of Hölderlin's destination and inner spirit: she is the unconscious knowledge that he must bring into his consciousness; and Muir accounts for Hölderlin's madness as being the result of his intuitive knowledge that "Diotima" was dead and that "without fear the lawless roads / Ran wrong through all the land" (*CP*, 66 - 68). [18] Hölderlin, like all men, must have a path through life. In other poems Muir retells the story of the fall of Troy ("Troy I" and "Troy II," later entitled "Troy" and "A Trojan Slave" [*CP*, 71 - 72]), while in "Ibsen" he imagines Sollness seeing other characters from Ibsen's plays in action as he falls from his tower. As is not uncommon in these poems of the 1930s, Muir is so completely serious in his consideration of his subject that he overlooks certain ludicrous lines: "Hilda Wangel down below / Now is no bigger than her hat" (*CP*, 75 - 76).

In spite of the second-hand images and language and of the literary topics, *Journeys and Places* includes poems in which Muir expresses personal experiences that he makes universal. Certainly this universality can be felt in the "visionary" aspects of "The Dreamt-of Place"; and it is particularly strong in Muir's references to his childhood. This first stanza of "The Mythical Journey" refers directly to his early years in the Orkney Islands and to places near the family farm: [19]

> First in the North. The black sea-tangle beaches,
> Brine-bitter stillness, tablet-strewn morass,
> Tall women against the sky with heads covered,
> The witch's house below the black-toothed mountain,
> Wave-echo in the roofless chapel,
> The twice-dead castle on the swamp-green mound,
> Darkness at noon-day, wheel of fire at midnight,
> The level sun and the wild shooting shadows.
>
> (*CP*, 62)

This poem also illustrates the mode of expression which Muir was developing and which, in later years, was to prove more appropriate than any other to his contemplative verse. It consists of an extended grammatical unit of coordinated periods, the coordination being fused with the length of the verse. Thus in "Darkness at noon-day, wheel of fire at midnight," the coordination is not merely grammatical but also linked to the natural break in the line, while the contrast of "darkness" and "fire" gives an intellectual balance to the verse. One reads through the stanza with judgment suspended, realizing only at the end that such an uncritical acceptance of images ranging from the starkly realistic to the fantastic has been the aim of the poet. Here the images embody his memories, in which he finds the origin of man's dream, "The living dream sprung from the dying vision, / Overarching all," where man "builds in faith and doubt his shaking house" (*CP*, 63).

Had Edwin Muir stopped writing in 1939, he would be remembered as a brilliant literary journalist who wrote promising poems and novels and translated important German novels, who was an advocate of modern literature to the larger reading public, and whose writings are illustrative of their age. However, Muir continued to write; and while the chronological divisions I have made in his work are not hard and fast (I have myself already crossed over them), 1940 can be put forward as the approximate date at which Edwin Muir the literary artist emerges. Although many of these pre-1940 poems are worth reading—and there is the fact that Muir himself retained almost all of them, with the exception of the *Chorus of the Newly Dead*, for his *Collected Poems*—on the whole their importance lies in their forming the background to the later verse, rather than in their intrinsic literary value.

CHAPTER 6

The Poet: Poems Written in the Late 1930s and the 1940s

THE poems in *The Narrow Place* (1943) and *The Voyage* (1946) indicate the measure of Edwin Muir's mature poetic ability and prepare the way for the verse of his last years.[1] I have suggested that the significant date in Muir's poetic development was 1939, when he realized that he was "a Christian, no matter how bad a one."[2] This realization appears to have removed some block to Muir's creativity, for although the post-1940 poems do not all reach the same level, the content and expression of individual poems are increasingly harmonious; so that, if there are still faults, they are generally outweighed by the new accomplishments in these poems.

I Poems Written before 1939

This gradual development is easy to see in *The Narrow Place* because it contains poems written before 1939. Most of these show a characteristically mechanical construction. Unable to acknowledge the full implications of his religious and philosophical ideas and hence unable to allow the thought to determine the structure, Muir falls back on rigid forms and meters that, although occasionally pleasing in themselves, usually restrict the meaning of the poem. This elaborately detailed construction is evident in "The Law." Muir addresses his "Law," his "Good," and his "Truth," which he does not "serve," "prize," or "seek," stressing the paradoxes by the use of parallels: lines 7 - 8 ("Where grace is beyond desert / Thanks must be Thanklessness") are answered by lines 13 - 14 ("If I could know ingratitude's / Bounds I should know gratitude"), and so on. The concluding stanza culminates in paradoxes:

> If I could hold complete
> The reverse side of the pattern,

> The wrong side of Heaven,
> O then I should know in not knowing
> My truth in my error.
>
> (*CP*, 106 - 107)

This mechanical rhetoric characterizes those rational, cerebral poems in which Muir turns his back on his meditative self. Even in "The Letter" (*CP*, 98)—which uses terms that derive from a "waking vision" that Muir described in *The Story and the Fable*[3]—the cerebration and the short-lined stanzas nullify the force of the actual experience.

Yet Muir is able to overcome this type of handicap, as "The Good Man in Hell" shows. The speaker of the poem wonders what would happen "if a good man were ever housed in Hell." If this man succumbed "to obvious hate," he would damn himself. On the other hand, if he could force "his praying tongue to run by rote,"

> Would he at last, grown faithful in his station,
>   Kindle a little hope in hopeless Hell,
> And sow among the damned doubts of damnation,
>   Since here someone could live and could live well?
>
> One doubt of evil would bring down such a grace,
>   Open such a gate, all Eden would enter in,
> Hell be a place like any other place,
>   And love and hate and life and death begin.
>
> (*CP*, 104)

Muir's religious predicament is indicated here by the fact that in 1938 he could only conditionally declare that "Faith" and "hope" might "bring down . . . grace," while his uncertain belief limits the measure of such "grace" and allows it merely to make "Hell be a place like any other place." Yet, partly because the idea of the poem is not difficult, Muir gives it full expression in the same rhymed quatrain form which had earlier caused obscurity and vagueness. Indeed, the simple diction and syntax and the unobtrusive speaker make the poem begin to meet the poet's own standard for poetic "greatness" as he stated it in *The Present Age*.[4]

The specifically theological subjects in these poems suggest that Muir's religious enlightenment in February 1939 was not unheralded. There are also several visionary poems in which Muir deduces religious—or at the least, psychological—meanings from specific incidents in his life. In his autobiography he writes about the landlord his family had known in the Orkneys. He was "a retired general," and Muir could "remember one soft spring day when the light seemed to be opening up the world after the dark winter; I must have been five. . . . The General was walking through the field below our house. . . . Now and then he raised his silver gun, the white smoke curled upward, birds fell, suddenly heavy after seeming so light; our cattle, who were grazing in the field, rushed away in alarm at the noise, then stopped and looked round in wonder at the strange little man. It was a mere picture; I did not feel angry with the General or sorry for the birds."[5] What in prose is a charmingly detailed account of a child's view of the world becomes in verse a farreaching evocation with mythic overtones.

> Early in spring the little General came
>   Across the sound, bringing the island death,
> And suddenly a place without a name,
>   And like the pious ritual of a faith,
>
> Hunter and quarry in the boundless trap,
>   The white smoke curling from the silver gun,
> The feather curling in the hunter's cap,
>   And clouds of feathers floating in the sun,
>
> While down the birds came in a deafening shower,
>   Wing-hurricane, and the cattle fled in fear.
> Up on the hill a remnant of a tower
>   Had watched that single scene for many a year,
>
> Weaving a wordless tale where all were gathered
>   (Hunter and quarry and watcher and fabulous field),
> A sylvan war half human and half feathered,
>   Perennial emblem painted on the shield
>
> Held up to cow a never-conquered land
> Fast in the little General's fragile hand.
>   (*CP*, 110 - 11)

The mutability of time is observed by the eternal, a conjunction that makes the field "fabulous." This word suggests a repeated tale of man's destroying other forms of life, yet nature in all her aspects is "never-conquered" and the human hand which holds the shield is "fragile." Muir may have been thinking of contemporary political matters (the English aristocrat among the Scottish peasants, for example), but the poem actually succeeds on a larger level in which the "never-conquered land" is neither an Orkney island nor Scotland, but rather nature herself. The poem celebrates the order implicit in nature and her inexhaustibility, that "dearest freshness deep down things" which is never lost, in spite of men's acts. Working out of an actual, personal experience, Muir expresses ideas unbounded by any one time or place, as he also does in "The Gate" (CP, 110), a poem about the initiation of children into adult life. Ihab Hassan, in his sensitive essay "Of Time and Emblematic Reconciliation," writes that in this poem "childhood ends, the gate swings open, and man finds himself within the prison. This is the burden of the song of innocence and experience."[6] The aesthetic value of this evocative poem is untouched by the fact that the terms of the poem apply equally well to many different types of initiation—sexual, religious, physical—which the maturing child encounters.

II   Universal Meanings Discovered in Specific Autobiographical Events

"The Gate" and other such poems are similar to earlier ones concerning childhood experiences, but after 1940 Muir almost consistently finds a general meaning, often on a mythical level, in his particular experiences.[7] He attains this universal meaning in most of the autobiographical poems, particularly those in The Voyage which are placed together: "Dejection," "Song of Patience," "Sorrow," "Comfort in Self-Despite," "The Transmutation," "Time Held in Time's Despite," "A Birthday," and, perhaps the most obvious, "The Myth" (CP, 150 - 52, 154 - 55, 157, 144).

The mythical element is also noticeable in "The Wayside Station," from The Narrow Place. This poem is based upon Muir's experiences in 1940 - 1941 when he was working at the Food Office in Dundee and traveling daily by train from St. Andrews with a change at Leuchars Junction. Each morning "at the wayside station" he watches "the smoke torn from the fumy engine / Crawling across the field" and the day "struggling" to be born, while "something here / Glimmers along the ground to show the seagulls / White on the furrows' black unturning waves." As the light increases he sees "the farmstead on the little hill" and imagines the scenes enacted as its inhabitants awaken, the farmer, the ploughboy, the "sad cattle."

> The lovers part
> Now in the bedroom where the pillows gleam
> Great and mysterious as deep hills of snow,
> An inaccessible land.

The sunlight increases as he muses:

> The wood stands waiting
> While the bright snare slips coil by coil around it,
> Dark silver on every branch. The lonely stream
> That rode through darkness leaps the gap of light,
> Its voice grown loud, and starts its winding journey
> Through the day and time and war and history.
>
> (*CP*, 92 - 93)

The poem places the events of each day against the background of "time . . . and history," while at the same time suggesting various universal myths. Thus the image of "the smoke torn from the fumy engine / Crawling across the field in serpent sorrow" alludes to the snake as a symbol of fertility and also anticipates the lines following it: "Flat in the east, held down by stolid clouds, / The struggling day is born and shines already / On its warm hearth far off." These terms suggest creation myths and explain the words, "something here / Glimmers along the ground": the "something" is life itself. The image of the sunrise as creation prepares the way for yet another idea, that of the lovers who must leave their "inaccessible land." The images are related by similar lighting effects, for the pillows "gleam" in the same way that the sun "glimmers" on the furrows, while the deeper relationship is also mythical: by their act of love the lovers have created the day. Actually such a meaning is the only one compatible with the concluding lines about the stream of time. Both thought and technique illustrate Muir's poetic advance by 1943. Unlike earlier poems there is no clumsy mechanism of dreams or reveries: the poet declares his ideas in a simple diction and in lines in which the varying lengths are determined by the content.

In other autobiographical poems Muir uses his personal moods as subjects. His "Song of Patience" shows a noteworthy matching of sound and sense and, because the lines imitate the rise and fall of the heartbeat, is one of the few poems in which the short lines seem entirely appropriate. "The Heart in its stations," he writes, "Has need of patience" as it holds "through night and day"

> Solitary monologue,
> Systole and diastole,
> Two surly words that say
> Each to each in the breast:
> 'Solid flesh, fluttering soul
> Troubles and fears, troubles and fears,
> Quick hope, long delay,
> Where is rest? Where is rest?'[8]
>
> (*CP*, 151)

The focus of the poem is broadened by the use of the image of the Stations of the Cross to imply the vicissitudes of life which the individual must endure (Muir used the same image, less skillfully, in *The Marionette*.)

III   *Other Topics*

But Muir does not write solely about his life: both *The Narrow Place* and *The Voyage* contain poems based on historical and legendary topics, and also on such new subjects for Muir as contemporary life, and in such new forms as the elegy. Some of Muir's earliest successes are found in those poems in which he expresses his ideas in the terms of a myth or legend, so that what is tentative or uncertain in his thought is covered over—or even animated—by the vitality of the old story. In the 1940s he continues to use such stories as frameworks; but with a clearer view of his intuitive ideas, he is able to invest in them his own idiosyncratic yet universal meanings.

"The Return of Odysseus" springs from Homer, but it focuses on Muir's concern with human absence and presence and also implies a universal meaning which relates to all readers. Muir describes Odysseus' house, where "lolling latches" allow it to be treated like "a public market," and he suggests the back-and-forth movement of Penelope's shuttle by the repetition of words:

> . . . She thought: 'Here I do nothing
> Or less than nothing, making an emptiness
> Amid disorder, weaving, unweaving the lie
> The day demands. Odysseus, this is duty,
> To do and undo, to keep a vacant gate

> Where order and right and hope and peace can enter.
> Oh will you ever return? Or are you dead,
> And this wrought emptiness my ultimate emptiness?'
>   (*CP*, 114)

Like mankind with its problems of daily existence, Penelope yearns for Odysseus, the long-awaited "good life." The optimistic conclusion parallels Muir's own ideas about life:

> She wove and unwove and wove and did not know
> That even then Odysseus on the long
> And winding road of the world was on his way.
>   (*CP*, 114)

Other legendary poems derive from the Bible and from Scottish history. "Moses" is a comment on contemporary life through the historical event of Jehovah's showing the land of Gilead to Moses; yet the poem includes more than one historical period, for the speaker—a collective voice—knows though he has not seen "The great disaster, exile, diaspora"; the trials of the Jews in the Near East; their checkered history in Europe; and the "trampling" of "That plot of ground pledged by the God of Moses." Muir's universalizing methods can be discerned in the opening lines of the poem, which refer initially to Moses:

> He left us there, went up to Pisgah hill,
> And saw the holiday land, the sabbath land,
> The mild prophetic beasts, millennial herds,
> The sacred lintel, over-arching tree,
> The vineyards glittering on the southern slopes,
> And in the midst the shining vein of water,
> The river turning, turning towards its home.
>   (*CP*, 129 - 30)

The appositives make the Jewish events universal: the specific holy day is amplified by the weekly day of rest; the "beasts" which are sacrificed become the "millennial herds"; and, more startling, "The sacred lintel" (a reference to the Passover ritual) is paralleled to the "over-arching tree," the pagan world-tree of Yggdrasill which figures in other poems.

"Robert the Bruce *To Douglas in Dying*" is based on the legend given in John Barbour's *The Bruce* (Book XX, lines 150 - 250), and, like earlier poems with literary origins, is in rhymed quatrains with a balladlike meter (*CP*, 115). Muir voices his fundamental idea that life before the Reformation had its order, explaining how through Christ's redemption of man a murderer who violated Church sanctuary in killing Comyn could have a place in that order. Muir unequivocally states that Christ's crucifixion alone redeems man's sin; yet significantly the poem is set in ancient times and has a speaker who is not the poet himself. These poems on legendary topics express more clearly, rather than develop, the themes of earlier poems, the difference being less one of direction than of quality, for Muir usually achieves a complete expression of his thought and does not confuse the main idea with glances at Nietzsche or Jung.

Perhaps one of the most obvious steps forward in these two collections is represented by those poems which concern contemporary events. Muir's long-sought-for mental balance and acceptance of himself at last made it possible for him to look at the world about him and, not retreating into myth, legend, or the fantasies of memory, to consider its meaning. Certainly he was not always successful in handling such subjects, nor did he write extensively on contemporary life; yet he achieved some notable successes in these poems.

One of them is "The Refugees." In *The Narrow Place* it is a fifty-two-line poem, although it was conceived and originally published as a sequence of dramatic monologues by a chorus and different speakers. The work resulted from Hermann Broch's visit with the Muirs in St. Andrews after Broch was released from an Austrian concentration camp; and the most powerful sections are those in which Muir literally transcribed his conversations with him. It is Broch's voice that is heard in the following, as comparison with the letters Broch wrote from St. Andrews and with Muir's diary, quoted in *The Story and the Fable*,[9] shows:

> To start awake at five each morning.
> The secret police came at five each morning
> To search the Jewish houses in Vienna.
> . . . .
> We rose and walked the streets, the streets were full of Jews.
> We went into the country, watched the ploughmen
> Stride carelessly behind their oxen, safe,
> The red fox creeping through the bushes, safe,
> The birds busy along the hedge-rows, safe,
> The white smoke rising from the farm chimneys.

> At nine we went back to our rooms.
> The house police kept hours, their work was finished,
> Done for the day at nine. [10]

The varying quality of the poem can be explained by reference to the
sources of each part, for the best sections are those in which Muir
writes about actual experiences that had been described to him, while
the weaker originate in his imagination—the sections, for example,
which purport to recount the emotions of a father and a mother upon
learning of the death of their son at the hands of the police.

All that Muir chose to keep of this long poem (which has affinities
with the *Chorus of the Newly Dead*) is a part of the final "Chorus."
The revised poem begins:

> A crack ran through our hearthstone long ago,
> And from the fissure we watched gently grow
> The tame domesticated danger,
> Yet lived in comfort in our haunted rooms.
> . . . .
> We did not fear
> A wrong so dull and old,
> So patiently told and patiently retold,
> While we sat by the fire or in the window-seat.
> > (*CP*, 95)

But "we now suffer . . . / Because we watched the wrong / Last too
long / With non-committal faces." The poet's despair throws him
back to his childhood beliefs in man's first sin and consequent damnation:

> For such things homelessness is ours
> And shall be others'. Tenement roofs and towers
> Will fall upon the kind and the unkind
> Without election,
> For deaf and blind
> Is rejection bred by rejection
> Breeding rejection,
> And where no counsel is what will be will be.
> > (*CP*, 96)

This fatalistic attitude does not accord with Muir's fundamental
beliefs, and he brings the poem—at the expense of its dramatic

force—into the framework of his optimistic philosophy only by ending it with the flat statement, "We must shape here a new philosophy."

Other poems with contemporary subjects include "The River," which, like Smetana's tone poem, "The Moldau," shows scenes enacted on the banks of the river of time; in the midst of present wartime disasters Muir looks toward the future good: "The stream flows on into what land, what peace, / Far past the other side of the burning world?" (*CP*, 93). In "Reading in Wartime" he asserts that Boswell's *Johnson* and Tolstoy's *Death of Ivan Ilych*—"Both being personal"—tell him more about "The meaning and the end / Of our familiar breath, / . . . / Than all the carnage can" (*CP*, 148). A somewhat different perspective is seen in "The Escape," a metaphysical poem about man's attempt to find God, his "enemy." Here the equivocal position of France in the 1940s provides the language, and the speaker crosses "the line between / The Occupied and the Unoccupied" territories only to find that the enemy's "work was everywhere" (*CP*, 126 - 28). In "Moses" there are references to contemporary pogroms: "the ghetto rising, / Toledo, Cracow, Vienna, Budapesth"; as well as to the laws about clothing to distinguish the Jews: "our people / In the wild disguises of fantastic time" (*CP*, 130). Yet, although there are other similarly oblique references, these poems rarely concern the war. Muir was actively engaged in war work in Edinburgh, but such activities were part of the "story" of his life, while his poems (which to him were synonomous with truth and meaning) came from and concerned the "fable" of his life and hence touched such "real" experiences only tangentially.

Both *The Narrow Place* and *The Voyage* contain elegies. "To J. F. H. (1897 - 1934)," the first poem in *The Narrow Place*, stands as a dedication for the entire volume and commemorates Muir's friend John Holms. Muir describes the experience of momentarily believing that Holms was alive and actually with him. He is certain of the validity of this psychic experience,[11] and, hoping that the reader might be similarly convinced, he moves from description and acknowledgment of the unreal nature of the vision to a treatment of it as real. Finally he offers his ultimate understanding:

> The clock-hand moved, the street slipped into its place,
> Two cars went by. A chance face flying past
> Had started it all and made a hole in space,
> The hole you looked through always. . . .
>
> (*CP*, 91 - 92)

The divisions of the poem—they are based on shifts in the poet's handling of his material—are not unlike those of earlier poems; but the more accomplished technique prevents the reader from being aware of these divisions, and the long lines, with a varying number of syllables and irregular rhymes, are typical of some of the best poems in *The Narrow Place*. Like them, too, this elegy shows what Elizabeth Jennings calls Muir"'s "quite new ability to use common and colloquial speech without in any way spoiling the dignity and austerity of his music."[12]

While "To J. F. H." is perhaps centered more on Muir's emotions than on Holms's death, "For Ann Scott-Moncrieff," the elegy in *The Voyage*, holds closer to the central subject. The poem commemorates the person who was "Ann much more / Than others are that or this," and who has now, in death, "come of age": she is "entirely Ann," although to Muir she remains "this unsetting star / That shines unchanged in my eye." The reconciliation is characteristically low-keyed: death is merely a lesson she, like everyone, must learn: "you lately learnt to die," he writes (*CP*, 156). In contrast to the poem about Holms, the record of a startling psychic experience, this calm, reflective poem is more on the order of a conventional elegy and is, as Joseph H. Summers declares, "not only a fine poem but one of the few modern personal elegies which is not actually embarassing."[13] The verse forms parallel the measured tone, for the poem is written in rhymed quatrains, grouped in three stanzas, whereas the more impassioned poem about Holms has only chance rhymes and a freer rhythmic pattern.

IV Developments of Familiar Themes and Subjects

While these poems on topics which were relatively new for Muir reveal his increasing poetic scope, poems on the subjects and themes of his earlier work make up the larger part of *The Narrow Place* and *The Voyage*. In them he expresses the ideas of earlier poems and other imaginative writings with clarity and force. These poems include the love poems, the philosophical poems concerning mutability, and, finally, the large group of poems which in one way or another make use of the journey-of-life theme.

A. The Love Poems

The love poems celebrate married love, fusing Platonic and Christian elements. Thus in the poem "On Seeing Two Lovers in the Street" Muir tells the lovers that they "are not two / Any more, but one," for they are "lost" in their love and "Nothing can find them / Until they awake / In themselves or take / New selves to bind them" (*CP*, 145 - 46). The same idea stands behind the "Song" in which he declares that love has isolated his beloved and himself from "life roll[ing] by in thunder" and left "this calm with you and me." In it he can hear "This tranquil voice of silence, yes, / This single song of two" (*CP*, 147).

The sequence of poems in *The Narrow Place* entitled "The Annunciation," "The Confirmation," and "The Commemoration" brings together Platonic and Christian concepts of love. In the first Muir "sing[s] the liberty . . . in this iron reign"

> Where each asks from each
> What each most wants to give
> And each awakes in each
> What else would never be,
> Summoning so the rare
> Spirit to breathe and live.
>
> (*CP*, 117)

The lovers, in giving of themselves, thus "magnify" their new life. In "The Confirmation" this rebirth is understood to result from the reuniting of beings who were originally one: "Yes, yours, my love," the poet declares, "is the right human face. / I in my mind had waited for this long, / Seeing the false and searching for the true" (*CP*, 118). In the third poem Muir contemplates the temporal and the eternal: the love he and his beloved have known creates immortality:

> How can one thing remain
> Except the invisible,
> The echo of a bell
> Long rusted in the rain?
> This strand we weave into
> Our monologue of two,
> And time cannot undo
> That strong and subtle chain. [14]
>
> (*CP*, 119)

The religiously significant titles suggest that as the love of Christ unites man to God, so earthly lovers create a "strong and subtle chain" on earth, the supernatural power of love influencing the consciousness of man even in succeeding generations.

B. *Mutability*

The realization that temporal, earthly love can be seen in terms of an immortal love is paralleled by an acceptance of the mutability of time. In the 1920s and 1930s Muir rebelled against the changes which time brought about and yearned for a perfect, changeless world; he also speculated on Nietzsche's ideas of a world in which all things reappear.

The problem is suggested in *The Voyage* by the short poem "The Rider Victory" (*CP*, 142), while in "The Window" Muir reconciles himself to the mutability that time brings; at the same time he creates (as Elizabeth Jennings has noted) "a personal and a cosmic vision."[15] He describes a circular window filled with stained-glass pictures; the changing light shines through them, creating different patterns within the constant one. He and his beloved are enthralled by the "changing marvels" of the window; and yet it gives a vision of the future that forces him to acknowledge what time will bring:

> . . . turning towards you I beheld
> The wrinkle writhe across your brow,
> And felt time's cap clapped on my head,
> And all within the enclosure now,
> Light leaf and smiling flower, was false,
> The great wall breached, the garden dead.
> (*CP*, 143)

The validity of this psychic experience is reinforced by the realistic details: the colored light has actually distorted the face of the poet's companion, just as time will bring wrinkles to that same face, and Time is thought of as being like the cap worn by a judge when he pronounces the death sentence or, perhaps, like some medieval torture instrument. Muir's response to this experience is tersely affirmative as he looks at the window again and sees that "Across the towering window fled / Disasters, victories, festivals." The actual scenes within the window provide the poet's reconciliation, for while time will bring "disasters," it also contains "victories" and "festivals."

A third poem about time, "The House," is not unlike Yeats's early lyric "The Song of the Old Mother," in which the loss of sexual vigor represents the passing of time; but Muir goes beyond such fin-de-siècle romanticism. In this "house" the "young and lusty" take their ease, while "the bent and the aged" work. A "little old woman" declares that the young have " 'all they want,' "

'But we have nothing but knowledge to chew,
Only that, and necessity.
These two maintain this niggardly house.

'For the young and the rich are ignorant
And never guess what they've yet to rue—
The lenten days when they will be
Servants like us of this tyrannous house.'
                                            (*CP*, 143 - 44)

The meaning devolves upon the word *lenten*: Muir realizes that there
is no reason to revolt against or resist the passage of time, for after
man's old age—his "lenten days"—will come the Easter resurrection
and immortality. Such "knowledge," along with "necessity," sup-
ports his life. This acceptance of the mutability of time in *The Voyage*
comes about at least in part because of Muir's revived Christian belief
and faith in man's deliverance from time, for they allow him to accept
time and its changes; and they account for the calm tone of the poems
in *The Voyage* and later collections.

C. *Poems Concerning the Journey-of-Life Theme*
     The remaining poems in these two collections of the 1940s relate to
the journey-of-life theme. In these poems Muir speculates on man's
origins, considers man's life on earth, and looks forward to man's existence after death. Although Muir reaches no consistent
philosophical belief in these poems, he progresses beyond his earlier
poems because he now accepts his intuitive ideas as valid without the
need of any sort of outside authority.
     As I have already pointed out, many of Muir's early poems can best
be described in Jungian terms, even though in these same poems the
poet, by using some reference to a dream or vision, appears to dis-
sociate himself from the theory suggested by the poem. One of the
major accomplishments of *The Narrow Place* and *The Voyage* is the
straightforward presentation of this material from the racial un-
consciousness. Thus in "The Face" and "The Grove" Muir considers
man's archetypal origins and the bestial elements which man has not
outgrown, thinking of his own face as "a smiling summer sea / That
sleeps while underneath from bound to bound / The sun- and star-
shaped killers gorge and play" (*CP*, 106). He manages to give a
mythical aspect to these "terrors" from man's past (and therefore still
in his unconscious) by using names—"sun[fish]" and
"star[fish]"—for their objective correlatives which suggest both the
eponyms and the actual objects.

This malevolent side of man's archetypal origins is also alluded to in "The Grove." Here Muir once more recounts the story of his (and all men's) journey through the "grove" of all past human life, through the bestial in man to the age of beasts, "where as we went the shadows wove / Adulterous shapes of animal hate and love." This journey is no casual matter: man can only reach "the crag and top the towering hill" by going through the "grove": that is, he must acknowledge and recognize his bestial origins and kinships if he wishes to progress (*CP*, 108 - 109). The good in man's past is the subject of "The Old Gods," an inverted sonnet addressed to the "goddess" whose cheeks are "slow hollowed by millennial tears." This is the anima, or great mother figure.

> Eternity marvels at your counted years
> And kingdoms lost in time, and wonders how
> There could be thoughts so bountiful and wise
>
> As yours beneath the ever-breaking bough,
> And vast compassion curving like the skies.
> (*CP*, 119 - 20)

Just as the bestial lives on in man, so are these "old gods" present; and man must recognize both the good and the evil in his human inheritance.

The title poem of *The Voyage* provides a picture of souls traveling to their temporal lives.[16] It expresses the idea that the individual's life recurs over and over and that the individual brings knowledge from past lives to the present life. Muir's voyagers do not know why they are on the seemingly endless water; they steer southward, and "The sun by day, the stars by night / Had only us to look upon" (*CP*, 136). Yet the "peace" of this voyage cannot be gainsaid, and the travelers "call a blessing" on it.

> And blessing, we ourselves were blest,
> Lauded the loss that brought our gain,
> Sang the tumultuous world to rest,
> And wishless called it back again.
> (*CP*, 138)

Yet though on the ship they are "sweetly as gods together bound," there is no escaping the inevitable birth; and the voyagers "gladly, blindly" step on earth, clutching "The dream and a truth." Again Muir asserts his belief in the unity of mankind, his simile "as gods" providing an explanation: all men are a part of the Deity in whom they share their prenatal life. "The Voyage" is closely related to Wordsworth's "Intimations Ode," but while Wordsworth is always theoretical (in spite of the objective images he uses), Muir is characteristically practical here, selecting his images for their psychological truth in the light of post-Freudian symbolism. The spiritual progress of the soul toward physical life is set forth in symbols generally accepted as describing fetal growth. This interpretation may appear incongruous with the high-flown idealism of the poem; yet actually Muir only roots his theories in basic physical truths. The symbols are not altogether consistent here and in other late poems; but once Muir's eclecticism is understood, "The Voyage" and others like it become startlingly contemporary presentations of traditional ideas.

On the whole Muir is less concerned in these poems of the 1940s with man's spiritual origins than with man's present, temporal life, a change in attitude that reflects his own personal circumstances after he was swept into a world of activity in 1941. His day-to-day work for the British Council was entirely beneficial to his verse-writing, for his involvement and successes in the world about him encouraged him (as I have already shown above) to take contemporary topics as subjects for his poems and to experiment with such new literary forms for him as the elegy. Certainly, too, the assurance of his later verse is due, at least in part, to his realization that he could play a successful role in the society in which he lived.

But nowhere in Edwin Muir's literary opus are there abrupt changes or about-faces, and the majority of the poems in *The Narrow Place* and *The Voyage* are on the topics and in the forms which Muir had used for the past two decades. Thus, for example, the title poem of *The Narrow Place* uses the comparison that he had explored in earlier poems of man's spiritual-physical growth and the individual's ascent of a mountain. The "narrow place" which man has reached in his upward climb is bare of vegetation, save for "one little wild half-leafless tree," under which man can yet find "such ease / As if it were ten thousand trees." In the last stanza an unidentified voice directs man to

> Sleep underneath the tree.
> It is your murdering eyes that make
> The sterile hill, the standing lake,
> And the leaf-breaking wind
> Then shut your eyes and see[.]
>
> (*CP*, 102)

Again Muir refers to the tree of life, Yggdrasill, under which man is in harmonious relationship with life and time, and where temporal eyesight is inferior to the inner light. Man's unconscious can and will protect him in "the narrow place."

D. *Poems Concerning Religious Faith*

Other poems reflect Muir's developing religious faith. "The Recurrence," for example, delineates Nietzsche's hopeless idea of eternal recurrence, but the conclusion of the poem puts forward the Christian view of life: that the temporal world is only a small part of man's eternal life.

> And the heart and the mind know,
> What has been can never return,
> What is not will surely be
> In the changed unchanging reign,
> Else the Actor on the Tree
> Would loll at ease, miming pain,
> And counterfeit mortality.
>
> (*CP*, 104)

The weakness of the poem comes from the strict division between its two parts: there are thirty-three lines of description of recurrence followed by thirteen lines of denial of recurrence. The vivid image of "Actor on the Tree" is obviously intended to balance the parts, but a reader who cannot accept the poet's evaluation of Christ may find the structure of the poem ill shaped to its thought.

Muir's evolving religious attitude is revealed most clearly in the last two poems of *The Narrow Place*. In "The Question" the poet addresses man's soul as if it were a hunting bird which finds it is itself "that strange quarry you scarcely thought you sought" and which, being "bought," can now "perch in pride on the princely hand, at home, / And there, the long hunt over, rest and roam." Man's actions thus bring him to the ultimate goal (*CP*, 122). Finally, in "The Day" Muir prays that, if "in the mind of God or book of fate" there is a pattern for his life, he may be given

> . . . clarity and love that now
> The way I walk may truly trace again
> The in eternity written and hidden way;
> Make pure my heart and will, and me allow
> The acceptance and revolt, the yea and nay,
> The denial and the blessing that are my own.
>
> (*CP*, 122)

Thus *The Narrow Place* ends with Muir recognizing that divine help will bring him to the order of life. This recognition influences many of the poems in *The Voyage*, although it is implicitly rather than overtly expressed. Yet a few poems in the 1946 collection state an incontrovertibly Christian point of view. Perhaps the most obvious example is "Thought and Image" (*CP*, 132 - 34). It concerns the relationship of the soul and the body, and Christ's meaning to them both. Muir thinks first of "the shaping Thought," born "Past time and space," and followed "on earth" by "the Image . . . wrought / Of water and of clay." Caught up with the earth, the Soul would have progressed onward to "its doom" had not, "It's said, . . . / God came and entered in the womb / And passed through the gate of birth." God lived and grew in the world, and "Wood, iron, herb and animal / His friends were till the testing day." But these four friends were to become enemies: "Then braced by iron and by wood, / Engrafted on a tree he died." The crucifixion was only a momentary defeat, for though "His body . . . was locked in stone" and "dust, lay with the dust,"

> All that had waited for his birth
> Were round him then in dusty night,
> The creatures of the swarming earth,
> The souls and angels in the height.
>   (*CP*, 134)

Yet even in this statement of Christian faith Muir tries not to commit himself, employing such phrases as "It's said" when he refers to the Incarnation. This refusal to hold an absolute, specific religious faith characterizes Muir's last poems, to which "Thought and Image" points the way.

But it would be misleading to stress the overt display of religion in *The Voyage*, for in many of its poems Muir either self-consciously turns away from religion or obscures the religious issues as much as possible. In "The Escape," written in a contemporary idiom, Muir presents God as man's enemy who "smile[s] and turn[s] his back" on man, allowing the horror and disorder of war to exist: as in a dream, the loved one takes the form of an enemy. Muir's faith is such that he does not doubt the existence of his God (the "enemy" is, above all things, real); and he understands the war to be the result of God's letting "brute indifference overawe / The longing flesh and leaping heart / And grind to dust the ancient law" (*CP*, 126 - 28). God is always present, even if His back is turned on man. The terms of reference seem to have been chosen deliberately to obscure the religious content, even though the symbolism by opposites is clear enough.

Similarly in "The Castle" the religious issue is at first hidden by the parablelike story. A besieged fortress falls through treachery, even while "Friendly allies" are "drawing near:"

> What could they offer us for bait?
> Our captain was brave and we were true. . .
> There was a little private gate,
> A little wicked wicket gate.
> The wizened warder let them through.

In the last stanza the castle spokesman speaks for himself:

> I will maintain until my death
> We could do nothing, being sold;
> Our only enemy was gold,
> And we had no arms to fight it with.
>
>   (*CP*, 129)

Of the many possible interpretations of this parable, the common denominator of them all is the idea that the castle-dwellers operate like the members of one body, each with its own function. One member may appear less important than another, yet all must unite to maintain the health of the whole, the failure of one causing the collapse of all. While the message here may concern the importance of the individual to the body politic, or to the body social, it may perhaps most reasonably have to do with the individual's own body, represented as the "castle." The poem then becomes a preacher's exemplum directed at animal lust and sensuality, forces against which man has "no arms," since in his original sin he was "sold" to these forces. Implicit in the poem is the Christian ethos.

Muir's religious attitude to life is most obvious in the emphasis he places on his vision of an ideal place where "all should change to ghost and glance and gleam, / And so transmuted stand beyond all change" ("The Transmutation" [*CP*, 154]). This ideal world also appears in "The Three Mirrors," in which each stanza mirrors a different place. The first and second reflect Muir's own past; the third is his projection of the future. In it "evil and good" are reconciled, and he can see there

> The world's house open wide,
> The million million rooms
> And the quick god everywhere
> Glowing at work and at rest,
> Tranquillity in the air,
> Peace of the humming looms
> Weaving from east to west,
> And you and myself there.
>
> (CP, 140 - 41)

The "world's house" with its "million million rooms" echoes Christ's promise of the many mansions in His Father's house, yet the "quick god" is hardly the Christian God, and the "humming looms / Weaving from east to west" have less reference to the Christian-Hebraic tradition than to the Three Fates with their distaff, spindle, and shears. "The Three Mirrors" typifies Muir's diffuse expression of his religious faith in *The Voyage*.

The outlines of Muir's essentially religious attitude—man must not merely live in accordance with an ethical, rational standard, but seek an ideal revealed to his soul, knowing always that he is an immortal spirit—are revealed by these poems. Muir recognizes the importance of this religious feeling as a background and a support for his verse and celebrates it in the last three poems of *The Voyage*, "A Birthday," "All We," and "In Love for Long." Although their short, rhymed lines resemble those of earlier, obscure poems, Muir overcomes such limitations through the judicious use of approximate rhymes and diction balanced between connotative and nonconnotative words. The common themes of the poems are acceptance and gratitude. In the first Muir gathers to his "heart"

> Beast, insect, flower, earth, water, fire,
> In absolute desire,
> As fifty years ago.

> Acceptance, gratitude:
> The first look and the last
> When all between has passed
> Restore ingenuous good
> That seeks no personal end,
> Nor strives to mar or mend.
>
> (CP, 157 - 58)

The "acceptance" of the second poem is of a slightly different order:

> All we who make
> Things transitory and good
> Cannot but take
> When walking in a wood
> Pleasure in everything
>
> . . . .
> To fashion the transitory
> We gave and took the ring
> And pledged ourselves to the earth.
>
> (*CP*, 158)

Since things of the spirit arise from the physical world, the artist is "pledged . . . to the earth"; yet while his work is "transitory," it also shares his spiritual nature. The third poem fittingly concludes Muir's spiritual growth in *The Voyage*, showing his new emphasis on faith rather than logic, and expressing, as Elizabeth Jennings writes, "with the utmost simplicity the credo of his life, the conviction that the world, however terrifying, brutal and tormented, is still 'a world of love' ":[17]

> I've been in love for long
> With what I cannot tell
> And will contrive a song
> For the intangible
> That has no mould or shape,
> From which there's no escape.
>
> (*CP*, 159)

Unable to name the object of his love, Muir gives examples of it; but actually "It is not even a name," for it "is all constancy." The deceptively vague, low-keyed rhetoric masks the fact that only through such words could Muir express himself.

> This love a moment known
> For what I do not know
> And in a moment gone
> Is like the happy doe
> That keeps its perfect laws
> Between the tiger's paws
> And vindicates its cause.
>
> (*CP*. 160)

The picture of the doe and the tiger in the last stanza, reminiscent of

Dante and of Eliot, and of various biblical passages, reconciles the opposing forces contrasted in *The Voyage.* In the initial poem, "The
Return," the separation of Odysseus and Penelope represents the opposition of mutability and permanence; in the final poem these forces
are reconciled in the male-female image of the tiger and the doe
which lie down together—resolving the contrast—in "happy happy
love."

V   *Summary*

In *The Narrow Place* and *The Voyage* Muir generally turns from
looking backward into man's history to looking forward to man's
future. He never stops believing that the archetypal self is a source of
knowledge, but his later poems show far less emphasis upon man's
duality than upon man's need for the aid of a spiritual power outside
himself. While in earlier poems he dismisses free will as a delusion, he
now sees man as capable of deciding his own future, at least to the extent of either following or not following God's way for him, although
man, lacking the ability to find his way unaided, must rely on the
spiritual power manifested in Christ. Muir recognizes that such an
idea contradicts modern psychology, the former foundation of his
thought; but rather than attempt to justify it by reasoning, he falls
back on religious faith. Relying thus on faith, he can ignore rational
logic, and consequently the intricate verbal tangles of earlier poems,
which reflected his tortured reasoning and made his poems excessive-
ly obscure, give way to a simpler, more straightforward presentation.
No specific poem marks this division between reasoning and faith,
or between the Christian and a-Christian poems. Simply, certain
poems in *The Narrow Place* show that Muir's attitude to life
resembles a Christian's, and other poems in *The Voyage* demonstrate
a Christian solution for metaphysical problems. In spite of the frequent use of biblical images, Muir only rarely refers explicitly to
Christ, even when he accepts Christian love as the solution to his
problems. This reticence characterizes his organic development, in
which there are no abrupt shifts in thought or changes in style.
Muir's images do not change in the later poems, but their meanings
grow to encompass the new emphasis in his thought. The most significant example of such an image or theme is that of the road: it continues to represent the good way for man, but Muir, having found his
own road, now writes about what to do on it. Instead of worrying over
his past or future, he accepts the present, content in his faith about

whatever may lie before him. Because he accepts life, he turns away from such ideas as that of all time being coexistent and that of the eternal recurrence. Similarly the tree of life, or Yggdrasill, ceases to hold his attention: he no longer rests under the tree, but rather looks at the tree from the road he is actively following.

CHAPTER 7

The Poet: Poems of the Last Years

E DWIN Muir's reputation as a poet ultimately rests on the poems in *The Labyrinth* (1949), *One Foot in Eden* (1956), and those poems first published in the posthumous *Collected Poems* (1960, 1963).[1] The understanding of the human condition expressed in these poems allows Muir to be compared to the Wordsworth of "Tintern Abbey," for, after a lifetime of spiritual development, he too knew "the power / Of harmony, and the deep power of joy," and was able to "see into the life of things." The value of these poems is due in part to the technique—the absolute mastery of the simple statement—but their peculiar strength comes mainly from Muir's integrated knowledge of his life and world. The simple, direct language is the appropriate medium for the traditional wisdom that is embodied in them, while both style and content link Muir with the poets of the past.

In the 1940s Muir gradually found that his rediscovered Christian faith allowed him to synthesize his experiences and intuitive ideas—the "story" and the "fable"—and his poems begin to be shaped by his Christian vision, even though the earlier influences are so much a part of his mature personality that they continue to exist side by side with his new outlook. Nietzsche, Freud, and Jung had taught Muir (in opposition to the other-worldly religion of his childhood) to keep man's physical, earthly life at the center of his philosophy; and hence when he turned back to Christianity, he now saw the link between God and man in the Incarnation ("the Word . . . made flesh") as the most important aspect of Christianity. Muir never altogether reconciled his religious, philosophical, and psychological views, and trying to balance such divergent attitudes brought about the stress in his poems upon paradox and relativity, qualities which make his verses surprisingly contemporary in spite of their traditional message and style.

In the later poems Muir knows what he wants to say; and instead of hoping to discover his meaning as he writes (as is often the case in the earlier poems), he is now able to shape his verse so that it will communicate his vision. This awareness of his poetic aims extends even to a concern with the total effect of his collections of poems. He always arranged his poems in their book form to achieve particular aims, but the thrust of his thought in his early years was so diffuse that this arrangement provides only incidental assistance to the critic. In these later collections in which the poems are shaped by the poet's integrated vision, the order of arrangement is so important that the reader should initially read both *The Labyrinth* and *One Foot in Eden* from beginning to end to gain the complete meaning of each.

I   The Labyrinth (*1949*)

The image of the labyrinth—a place of blind passages which obscure the way through the maze—in the title poem provides the organizational pattern of this collection, for Muir places poems that are straightforward in meaning next to those that are misleading so that the reader will stumble along as though he were in a maze. Yet behind each group of poems lies the truth of the labyrinth: that being man-made, its mystery can be resolved by man.

A number of critics consider this collection and various poems in it to be highpoints in Muir's poetic achievement, but no one has drawn attention to the structural use of the sonnets in the overall shape of the collection. The sonnet which begins the collection, actually preceding the title poem, is highly significant. Entitled "Too Much," it is an English sonnet in which the poet stresses the fact that man has a path through his life and through time. No matter that "Hour and place / Are huddled awry, at random teased and tossed, / Too much piled on too much, no track or trace," for the poet can

> . . . . . . watch the old
> Worn saga write across my years and find,
> Scene after scene, the tale my fathers told,
> But I in the middle blind, as Homer blind,
>
> Dark on the highway, groping in the light,
> Threading my dazzling way within my night.
>   (*CP*, 163)

Although the labyrinth image incorporates by its nature alternating moods of doubt and assurance, the key position of this declaration of "a way" asserts that the confusion of the labyrinth is temporal and that the blindness of the individual is only his limitation, and prevents only him from seeing the true world which lies all about him. Interestingly enough, the same image of blindness also figures in the initial sonnet of *One Foot in Eden*: in it Milton must only take "one step more" for "his unblinded eyes" to see "the fields of Paradise" (*CP*, 207).

This opening sonnet provides the touchstone of truth for the reader when he proceeds to those poems which, like "The Labyrinth," cast doubt upon man's hope of finding a path. As with earlier poems employing a myth, one must again remember the story, for Muir's symbols not only stand for something else (here the "labyrinth" can be said to represent psychological or religious or moral confusion) but are significant in their own right. As Christopher Wiseman has noted in reference to this poem, "the symbols are not reminders of meaning as much as sources of meaning, striving to define themselves."[2] The import of the poem depends upon one crucial fact: that Daedalus constructed the maze in order to incarcerate the Minotaur, and that Theseus was able to find his way through it. The speaker of the poem is Everyman-Muir in the guise of Theseus; he has killed the beast and "emerged . . . from the labyrinth," yet "There have been times when I have heard my footsteps / Still echoing in the maze. . . ." He tells himself that " 'This / Is the firm good earth. All roads lie free before you.' "

> But my bad spirit would sneer, 'No, do not hurry.
> No need to hurry. Haste and delay are equal
> In this one world, for there's no exit, none,
> No place to come to, and you'll end where you are,
> Deep in the centre of the endless maze.'
>   (*CP*, 164)

Following his usual pattern of statement and contrast, Muir then turns to the "real world" which he "touched . . . once, / And now shall know . . . always." Intuitive knowledge is the source of his faith:

> . . . once in a dream or trance I saw the gods
> Each sitting on the top of his mountain-isle,

. . . .
> And their eternal dialogue was peace
> Where all these things were woven, and this our life
> Was as a chord deep in that dialogue,
> As easy utterance of harmonious words,
> Spontaneous syllables bodying forth a world.
>
> (*CP*, 165)

This intuitive knowledge echoes the truth which "Too Much" expresses; but man, in his fallen condition, is not privileged to live with such assurance constantly before him and must endure "the lie, / The maze, the wild-wood waste of falsehood, roads / That run and run and never reach an end, / Embowered in error." Yet the poem does not present a simple contrast between the worlds of "truth" and "illusion" because the poet, secure though he is in his knowledge of the eternal truth, realizes that in the shadow-world of temporal life there are no Absolutes. The last stanza makes this realization clear:

> Oh these deceits are strong almost as life.
> Last night I dreamt I was in the labyrinth,
> And woke far on. I did not know the place.
>
> (*CP*, 165)

Muir deliberately turns back upon an absolute belief and creates an enigma in order to stress the reality of each of the worlds which man encounters in his daily life.

"The Labyrinth" shows Muir not only expressing his ideas with a subtle balance, but also shaping his verses with complete mastery. As Elizabeth Hubermann points out, "Critics have uniformly admired what Muir called the 'deliberately labyrinthine' first sentence, which spins its intricate system of dependent clauses and parentheses through thirty-five lines of freely handled blank verse. The 'remarkable, sustained syntax' here 'winds and turns upon itself. . . ,' notes Harvey Gross in *Sound and Form in Modern Poetry*. 'The syntax *acts out* the journey of Theseus.' "[3] And after an elaborate analysis of the poem, Christopher Wiseman writes that "the prosody of the poem is highly expressive, itself symbolising dream and the time-space dislocation through irregularity, and actuality through insistent regularity. . . . [M]etre and syntax are . . . an organic part of the poem's movement in and out of actuality and dream."[4]

The four poems "The Way," "The Return," "The West," and

"The Journey Back" center on the way that man must follow through the labyrinth of life. The first stresses that man must always move forward, for though he may want to "travel back," "*None goes there, none*" (*CP*, 166). In the second, the poet looks with longing at the path he has traversed; it is now like a house or walled city in which lie his "Childhood and youth and manhood all together, / And welcome waits, and not a room but is / My own, beloved and longed for." But there can be no return, for he must "turn aside and take the road / That always, early or late, runs on before" (*CP*, 167). In "The West" Muir uses the ancient equation of the sunset and the end of man's physical life to suggest that although "from the east newcomers constantly / Pour in among us, mix with us, pass through us, / And travel towards the west," there is "A west beyond the west," and "the little earthen mound" (that is, the grave) is only what man's limited view lets him see of this "west." Yet even with such knowledge, men recognize that "this is a land, and we say 'Now', / Say 'Now' and 'Here', and are in our own house" (*CP*, 168).

This section concludes with "The Journey Back," a seven-part poem which reproduces in miniature the overall labyrinthine structure of the collection. In essence the poem summarizes ideas about "the way" which are given in preceding poems. In the first section Muir is concerned with finding the origins of man's road: he looks back into his own life, past his "father's farmer hands," past the primitive lives associated with "The savage keep, the grim rectangular tower / From which the fanatic neighbour-hater scowls," and realizes that he is both "Victor and victim, hapless Many in One" and that "In all these lives I have lodged, and each a prison." This accumulation of lives (the poem might well be called a description of the racial unconscious) would be unending, were it not that the poet knows "that some day / . . . I shall find a man who has done good / His long lifelong and is / Image of man from whom all have diverged" (*CP*, 169 - 70). Peter Butter aptly calls this "a characteristically humble reference to Christ . . . [who] must be found within time, not by escaping from it."[5]

The second and third poems take the poet even farther back in time, to the age when "Before the word was said/With animal bowed head/I kept the laws" (*CP*, 171). The "word" is the Logos or Christ, and the reference prepares the way for the grief of the poet when he contemplates "the poor child of man" in primitive ages who, "Not knowing the resurrection and the life," was "Shut in his simple recurring day" (*CP*, 172). The fourth poem is one of the most labyrinthine in meaning: it suggests that there is an essence in life which, being a part of all things, lies beyond the poet's power to name. Emphasis is placed on the reality of the world and earthly time, for Muir never despises the phenomenal world which man's senses recognize. Such an idea is in accord with the meaning of the following poem: that it is in this world and this time that a blessing—"the kingdom"—will come (*CP*, 173).

The sixth poem in the sequence concerns the "right way" to live and appropriately takes the form of a lyric with clear, mellifluous sounds. On this road "music's self itself has buried there," and the movement of life along its way provides the music itself.

> This is the other road, not that we know.
>
> This is the place of peace, content to be.
> All we have seen it; while we look we are
> There truly, and even now in memory,
>
> Here on this road, following a falling star.
> (*CP*, 174)

But even as the poet makes this assertion, he prepares to return to the phenomenal world; and in the final poem he accepts the fact that man in his earthly life cannot know either the " 'starting-point' " or the "end" of his journey.

> There's no prize in this race; the prize is elsewhere,
> Here only to be run for. There's no harvest,
> Though all around the fields are white with harvest.
> There is our journey's ground; we pass unseeing.
> But we have watched against the evening sky,
> Tranquil and bright, the golden harvester.
> (*CP*, 175)

The labyrinth of man's life has perhaps more dark passages than bright, yet over all is the golden glow of the evening sun, promising a release from the labyrinth.

While this first passageway in the labyrinth shows a way out for man, the following section immediately casts him into a maze of dark bypaths and cul-de-sacs. The four poems "The Bridge of Dread," "The Helmet," "The Child Dying," and "The Combat" provide literal and metaphorical statements about man's fears and doubts. "The Bridge of Dread" is a painfully graphic description of fear ("you watch your footsteps crawl / Toadlike across the leagues of stone" [*CP*, 176]). It is followed by the description of a man whose "helmet on his head / Has melted flesh and bone / And forged a mask instead / That always is alone" (*CP*, 177). "The Helmet" concerns the individual who is cut off from other men by his fears and terrors and recalls Muir's study of a similar figure, the character Hans, in *The Marionette*. "The Child Dying" may have been derived from Goethe's "Erlkönig," but the child speaking here does not resist death and indeed speaks to the father after he dies: "My hand in yours no more will change, / Though yours change on . . . / . . . / I did not know death was so strange" (*CP*, 178).

This dark section of poems ends with one of Muir's best-known pieces, "The Combat." In it two fabulous beasts battle. One is violent—"Body of leopard, eagle's head / And whetted beak, and lion's mane, / And frost-grey hedge of feathers spread / Behind"—and the other is passive—"A soft round beast as brown as clay; / All rent and patched his wretched skin; / A battered bag he might have been." The combat has no end:

> And now, while the trees stand watching, still
> The unequal battle rages there.
> The killing beast that cannot kill
> Swells and swells in his fury till
> You'd almost think it was despair.
>   (*CP*, 179 - 80)

Daniel Hoffman describes this poem as "a horrible nightmare of defenselessness in unmitigated battle with aggressive power, yet all but victorious in its capacity for eternal suffering. . . . There is something indefinably terrifying in this vision of struggle without end between the unappeasably destructive element and the undefeatable passivity of pure suffering." Muir's technique here illustrates the influence Kafka had on him, for while there are obviously allegorical meanings within the poem (its terms must have been chosen for their suggestiveness), at the same time the two creatures are no more than what they appear to be and, as Hoffman remarks, "simply act out their natures."[6] It is perhaps helpful to remember that Muir spoke at length in his lecture "The Politics of *King Lear*," delivered about the time he wrote this poem, on Shakespeare's use of animal traits to characterize humans,[7] for clearly the poem is a metaphorical statement of the individual's conflicts both within himself and in his life in the outer world. There seem to be indeed an endless number of opposing qualities represented here, and the grotesque animals have all the evocative powers of some iconographical emblem.

One might consider "The Intercepter," which follows "The Combat," to provide a guide to its meaning: the "intercepter" is simply the other part of the poet's divided self, who may be either friend or enemy, "Betrayer, [or] saviour from disgrace" (*CP*, 180 - 81). There is merit in such a reading; but the second poem is much more limited than the first and is actually more akin to the ninth poem in the *Variations on a Time Theme,* in which the "other part" of the poet is named "Indifference."[8] Similarly "Head and Heart" depicts the divided self in whom "what we know and what we see / Are separate as head and heart" (*CP*, 181).

The next group of poems shares topical references and contemporary language and reminds one that twentieth-century man lives within the labyrinth. Both "The Interrogation" and "The Border" (*CP*, 182 - 83) employ images drawn from political situations in Europe in the 1940s, the first poem being a particularly suggestive picture of time stopped. The speakers have been captured by the enemy patrol; and now, while "careless lovers in pairs go by, / Hand linked in hand, wandering another star," the interrogation goes on and on, until "We are on the very edge, / Endurance almost done."

In "The Good Town" Muir recalls a town he had known before the war (Prague was probably in his mind), compares it with what it has become, and attempts to account for the monstrous transformation. The town was once "Known everywhere, with streets of friendly neighbours, / Street friend to street and house to house"; and while it was not perfect, yet "Kindness and courage can repair time's faults, / And serving him breeds patience and courtesy" (*CP*, 183 - 84). Now there are only "mounds of rubble, / And shattered piers, half-windows, broken arches"; the "people have been scattered, or have come / As strangers back."

> No family now sits at the evening table;
> Father and son, mother and child are *out*,
> A quaint and obsolete fashion. In our houses
> Invaders speak their foreign tongues. . . .
> . . . .
> . . . If you see a man
> Who smiles good-day or waves a lordly greeting
> Be sure he's a policeman or a spy.

We know them by their free and candid air.
                    (*CP*, 184 - 85)

Although the change was directly caused by "these two wars," yet it seems to have come from "an endless source, / Disorder inexhaustible, strange to us, / Incomprehensible."

> What is the answer? Perhaps no more than this,
> That once the good men swayed our lives, and those
> Who copied them took a while the hue of goodness,
> A passing loan; while now the bad are up,
> And we, poor ordinary neutral stuff,
> Not good nor bad, must ape them as we can,
> In sullen rage or vile obsequiousness.
>   (*CP*, 186)

The truly contemporary quality of the poem comes not only from the subject but also from Muir's understanding of the forces of modern society, which are beyond the control of individuals.

> Say there's a balance between good and evil
> In things, and it's so mathematical,
> So finely reckoned that a jot of either,
> A bare preponderance will do all you need,
> Make a town good, or make it what you see.
> But then, you'll say, only that jot is wanting,
> That grain of virtue. No: when evil comes
> All things turn adverse, and we must begin
> At the beginning.   .   .   .
>   (*CP*, 186)

Knowing that life is lived within the labyrinth, Muir offers no formula for making the world a better place, only the knowledge that one must live within time, working for good in the present moment and not in some future world order. Although free of any specific political comment, the poem is clearly aimed at the Communist doctrine of the end justifying the means and at the idea that revolution will bring change.[9]

This group of poems also includes "The Usurpers" which, according to Peter Butter, "can be imagined" to be spoken by "the young Gestapo men" who, growing up in a spiritual and moral vacuum, could "still the ancestral voices" and "dare do all we think,/Since there's no one to check us, here or elsewhere" (*CP*,

187 - 88). Thus, according to Butter, they "have won a kind of freedom, which is in fact illusory and at the opposite pole to the boundless freedom and union of which Muir wrote elsewhere. . . . They live in light and darkness only, in the temporal only, not seeking the place of vision where light and darkness meet, the 'place of images.' "[10]

These poems bring the first half of *The Labyrinth* to a close: in them the poet writes mainly of the shadows of the labyrinth, even though he knows that there is a way out. While the second half does not altogether contrast with the first, its poems provide more concrete instances of the light which penetrates into the labyrinth. Again an English sonnet introduces the section. In "Too Much," the initial sonnet, the poet declares that he "did not bargain for so much" (*CP*, 163). Here in "The Bargain" he writes, "I strike the bargain, since time's hand is there; / But having done, this clause I here declare." "This clause" refers to the following poems in which the way out of the labyrinth is described. In short, though "Time gave and took away," there are yet ways for man to overcome time and its changes (*CP*, 188). The subtle balance of Christian and pagan ideas in these poems shows that Muir held simultaneously both Christian and non-Christian beliefs and reminds one of his remark to his wife as he was taken to the hospital in his final illness, " 'There are no absolutes, no absolutes.' "[11]

Thus the next poem is "Oedipus," another dramatic narrative. In "The Usurpers" the young Gestapo men arrogantly and erroneously declare, "We are free"; and this misconception causes their downfall. Oedipus, on the contrary, knows that his life depends upon "That predestined point / Where three paths like three fates crossed one another"; that, acting in all innocence, he had to do what he did; and that he must now pay the price. Man must accept that which he cannot understand, knowing only

> That all must bear a portion of the wrong
> That is driven deep into our fathomless hearts
> Past sight or thought; that bearing it we may ease
> The immortal burden of the gods who keep
> Our natural steps and the earth and skies from harm.
> (*CP*, 190 - 91)

Such altruistic concern in the love for others lies behind the three lyrics "Circle and Square," "Love's Remorse," and "Love in Time's

Despite"; these three poems also serve as a transition into the overtly Christian poems of the collection (*CP*, 191 - 93).

The first of these poems is "Soliloquy." Its speaker is a retired
Greek merchant who ponders the events in his life and their
significance. He witnessed the Crucifixion, and he has "thought of
death, / And followed Plato to eternity." Now, however, in old age,
although he realizes "there's no bargain you can drive with time"
(Muir sounds again the theme of the sonnet beginning the section),
he has learned to cherish life and the "sight . . . of the
original / That is myself" which has been granted to him from time
to time (*CP*, 195 - 96). Thus, at the end of his life,

> Light and praise,
> Love and atonement, harmony and peace,
> Touch me, assail me; break and make my heart.
> (*CP*, 197)

Although the character disclaims Christianity, the words put in his
mouth are the words of Christianity, for Muir clearly wants both the
faith of the Christian and the ideals of the virtuous pagan.

Again there follow two lyrics, "The Absent," a celebration of the
immortality of those who have gone on before and who are yet ever
present in the living (*CP*, 197), and "The Visitor," a plea to
"Brother and sister, wife and son," for solitude that will allow the
poet to receive his "ghost" (*CP*, 198), that Platonic "original" of
whom the Greek merchant spoke in his "Soliloquy." These two
poems lead to "The Transfiguration" (*CP*, 198 - 200), a dramatic
monologue spoken by those who beheld the Transfiguration of
Christ. Peter Butter provides an illuminating comment on this
poem by studying its relationship to traditional "Christian thought
about the Transfiguration"; he quotes a letter by Muir which shows
that the poet knew nothing of the accepted teaching that "[t]he
body is an essential and integral part of man [and] shall rise at the
last day and share in the glory of Heaven. In the Transfiguration
the true nature of the body, temporarily obscured, is revealed."[12]
Thus Muir's equation of the Transfiguration with a return to primal
order where "all / Was in its place" is well within the bounds of
Christian doctrine, while at the same time proving the validity of
the poet's intuitive knowledge. Equally important for the wayfarer
through the labyrinth of earthly life is the promise which is a part of
Christ, that *in time*

> . . . he will come, Christ the uncrucified,
> Christ the discrucified, his death undone,
> His agony unmade, his cross dismantled—
> Glad to be so—and the tormented wood
> Will cure its hurt and grow into a tree
> In a green springing corner of young Eden,
> . . . .
> . . . . and the betrayal
> Be quite undone and never more be done.
>   (*CP*, 200)

Christ, then, is the way; and in Him is the end of the earthly labyrinth. Yet for all of this positive faith, Muir refuses to limit himself to it alone: even this affirmative passage contains such disclaimers as "it's said" and "some say" in reference to Christ.

These disclaimers appear, however, to be more for the purpose of bringing in other beliefs than for limiting the Christian faith, since the collection is brought to a close by three poems, "The Debtor," "Song," and "The Toy Horse" (*CP*, 200 - 203), in which love is stressed as the answer to man's problems: the refrain of "Song" is the simple theme, "Love gathers all." This mood of love and acceptance shines through the enigmatic lines of the last poem in the collection, "The Toy Horse." Muir is too honest to end his "labyrinth" with any easy, clear statement; and this poem—K. L. Goodwin and T. S. K. Scott-Craig have studied it in detail[13]—fittingly brings the collection to an end with the image of a child's toy that has some unexplained meaning, even though, as Scott-Craig notes, "the poem has a positive but not blatant Christian orientation." Perhaps the most significant term in the poem is the last line: the poet addresses the "Dumb wooden idol" which has led the "pilgrimage / Between the living and the dead" and which now shines "in your golden age" (*CP*, 203). Dark though the labyrinth may be, the golden light of the millennium lies at the end of man's way through it.

In *The Labyrinth* Muir unites themes, subjects, and expression to achieve completely integrated poems. Underlying the organic unity of the whole volume is the poet's vision of human life. Indeed, the value of the poems lies in this essentially moral vision, and *The Labyrinth* clearly shows that its author must be ranked with those other great poets whose sense of morality is inseparable from their art.

II One Foot in Eden *(1956)*

Unlike *The Labyrinth*, with its single unifying image, *One Foot in Eden* has two separate parts, the title serving merely to hint at the poet's general attitude to life. The poems in the first part have as their common basis the belief that every individual life has a certain universality, so that the experience of the individual is the experience of all. These poems are arranged according to the chronology of their subject matter, beginning with the seven days of creation and going up to the twentieth century. The more diverse poems in the second part are generally attempts to examine different human types and human situations and to find the metaphysical meaning of each. In both sections the sonnets again provide the structural skeleton by announcing themes and signaling changes of attitude.

A. *Part One*

One Foot in Eden begins with the sonnet "Milton," one of Muir's best poems. Completely natural and unforced in tone, meter, or rhyme, it achieves a dignity and absolute conviction which make it worthy of its subject. The force of the poem arises from the reality of Muir's vision of Milton as the blinded poet who, tormented by "the devilish din" and "the steely clamour known too well / On Saturday nights in every street in Hell," never lost his belief in the "Paradise" which lies at the end of man's journey: he had only to take "a footstep more" and "his unblinded eyes" would see "far and near the fields of Paradise" (*CP*, 207). This vision of Milton is historically faithful: the reference to "the steely clamour" actually originates in Milton's own reference to the brawling Cavaliers outside his window ("the barbarous dissonance / Of Bacchus and his revellers," *Paradise Lost*, VII, 32 - 33). At the same time this vision enables Muir to present his own metaphysical beliefs, particularly his idea that man's ultimate goal is not only accessible but even nearby at all times.

The beliefs implied or stated here provide the light in which to view the succeeding poems, for whatever they may say, "Milton" states the final truth. In the first three poems, "The Animals," "The Days," and "Adam's Dream" (*CP*, 207 - 12), Muir describes Paradise before man's fall, for to Muir Eden is the primal world of archetypes and thus both the beginning of all things and the end to which they strive to return. These poems are rich in symbolic images that have a significance of their own, independent of the meaning of the poem as a whole. In the catalogue of created things given in "The Days," the phrase "The lion set / High on the banner, leaping into the sky" (*CP*, 209) designedly evokes ideas of Scottish history, of heraldry and armies, of the moral qualities of bravery and courage—and of the lion itself, the totem in its own right.

These poems also demonstrate Muir's fantastic range, for, as Huberman points out, " 'The Days' narrates the entire history of the Creation from the first through the seventh days,"[14] while "Adam's Dream" gives the story of man's life after the expulsion from the garden, "a great vision of pity and compassion," according to J. R. Watson, who considers the poem to have been suggested by Milton.[15] In this phantasmagoric capsulation of time and space Adam sees the growing numbers of men, "a mechanical / Addition without meaning, joining only / Number to number in no mode or order, / Weaving no pattern" (*CP*, 211); yet when he comes closer to this swelling crowd, he realizes that "They were about some business strange to him / That had a form and sequence past their knowledge." Unsatisfied by this "illustrated storybook of mankind / Always a-making, improvised on nothing," he tries to hail them and remembers then that they are his children, condemned to act without knowledge because of his transgression:

> . . . [He] took their hands
> That were his hands, his and his children's hands,
> Cried out and was at peace, and turned again
> In love and grief in Eve's encircling arms.
> (*CP*, 212)

This theme is continued in "Outside Eden," the poet's musing on man's life outside Eden in a state of sin. Both Milton and Wordsworth stand close behind the poem: in describing Adam's fall, Muir echoes Milton's description of the expulsion of Lucifer from Heaven (*Paradise Lost*, I, 44 - 45): Muir's Adam and Eve "fell and fell through all the fall / That hurled them headlong over the wall" (*CP*, 213). And in accounting for man's tolerance of this world of sin, when he should be able to remember the joys of Eden, Muir recalls an image from Wordsworth's "Intimations Ode": that man is like a child distracted by his foster-mother nature so that he does not remember his heavenly origins. Thus Muir writes that while "The simple have long memories[,] / Memory makes simple all that is." The world may be as "wrong and clear / As the crude drawings of a child," yet it is "more dear / Than geometrical symmetry." Man, who must "[stand] on earth, looking at heaven," is blessed in possessing such simplicity and lack of comprehension (*CP*, 214).

Muir next presents poems about man in the heroic age of the Greeks, bringing together in several of them his fascination with Greek legend and his ever-developing Christian faith. In "Prometheus" the god speaks from his chains, describing the world that changes about his changeless self from his knowledge that only in Christ can he find release from time:

> A god came down, they say, from another heaven
> Not in rebellion but in pity and love,
> Was born a son of woman, lived and died,
> And rose again with all the spoils of time
> Back to his home. . . .
> If I could find that god, he would hear and answer.
>   (*CP*, 215 - 16)

Often in these poems Christian virtues provide the answers man needs, as in "Orpheus' Dream," where Orpheus' hope of rescuing Eurydice is accompanied by "Forgiveness, truth, atonement, all / Our love at once" (*CP*, 217). Telemachos (in "Telemachos Remembers") describes his mother's unceasing weaving (this image always fascinated Muir), speculating on what her tapestry might have become had it been finished, but not realizing that temporal man can never bring his deeds to a conclusion and "Not knowing she wove into her fears / Pride and fidelity and love" (*CP*, 219 - 20). "The Charm" emphasizes the concept of the "fortunate fall," the theological rationalization that only after man fell from grace could he know the virtues of pity and compassion and receive the Incarnate God in Christ. To live without knowing these virtues ("all the charities, unborn, / Slept soundly in his burdened breast") is to live as though enchanted by the charm which takes "All memory and all grief away" and allows "indifference" to grow (*CP*, 218 - 19).

But some of these poems are difficult to reconcile to any theology or philosophy. "The Other Oedipus," for example, presents the

blind king with "his serving-boy and his concubine"; the three have
forgotten all of their tragic story and, free of time and space, have
regained a childlike happiness so that they live in "a day"

> Without a yesterday or a to-morrow,
> A brightness laid like a blue lake around them,
> Or endless field to play or linger in.
>
> (*CP*, 217)

Muir's handling of the story shows a novel approach, but as in the
Oedipus poem in *The Labyrinth*[16] Muir is again describing man as a
pawn of fate, an innocent victim who can regain his happiness once
he forgets what time and destiny forced him to do.

These Greek poems end with a sonnet. "The Heroes" points out
that these heroes looked forward to no heaven, "no Elysium"; indeed "They were stripped clean of feature, presence, name"; and
yet from their "namelessness" there comes "that strange glory" surrounding them (*CP*, 220). Muir accepts the phenomenal world and
man's temporal life; but he is true to his Platonic convictions at the
same time and insists that the abstract virtue outlasts both the deed,
the doer of the deed, and the world in which it is accomplished.

From the world of the Greeks Muir turns to the Hebraic-
Christian world, considering "Abraham" (*CP*, 221) and, in "The
Succession," other Jewish patriarchs who, being the chosen people
("we drew the enormous lot"), must search "through the
generations" (*CP*, 221 - 22). "The Road," although couched in the
familiar terms of the journey-of-life image and not actually referring to the Jews, gains its meaning from the place it occupies in this
sequence: coming after the two specifically Jewish poems, the statement that the travelers hear, " 'There was another road you did not
see,' " must refer to the rejection of Christ by the Jews and their
continuing hope for the Messiah (*CP*, 223). This sonnet ends the
Old Testament poems and introduces those poems which have to do
with "another road," the way of the New Testament.

These nine poems pose several problems: they are undeniably
Christian in attitude, with few of the reservations of earlier poems;
most of them were published in periodicals before being included in
this collection; and yet Muir omitted four of them—"The Christmas," "The Son," "Lost and Found," and "The Lord"—from the
Collected Poems. The omission is all the more important in view of
the fact that Muir excluded so very few poems from this volume;
and the explanation he offered to T. S. Eliot, the publisher of the

Collected Poems, "I have decided to leave out four of the religious poems, which seem to me now to be quite inadequate,"[17] may be somewhat ingenuous. The omitted poems show technical limitations; but Muir appears to have been intent, even at this stage in his life, to hold on to the widest possible religious belief. To this end he cut out enough poems to prevent the *Collected Poems* from having a predominantly Christian slant. Again the sonnets provide a framework: the first four poems—"The Annunciation" (*CP*, 223 - 24), "The Christmas" (*OFE*, 38), "The Son" (*OFE*, 39), and "The Killing" (*CP*, 224 - 25)—recount events in the life of Christ; they conclude with the sonnet "Lost and Found" (*OFE*, 43), an affirmation of faith. The enigmatic and paradoxical "Antichrist" (*CP*, 226) follows like a countertruth, being balanced by another affirmative sonnet, "The Lord" (*OFE*, 45). The sequence ends with two poems concerning the Christian faith in the modern world, "One Foot in Eden" (*CP*, 227) and "The Incarnate One" (*CP*, 228).

In "The Annunciation" Muir creates an attractive visual image of "the angel and the girl" looking at one another in a "deepening trance / As if their gaze would never break." The poet finds in this traditional scene his own particular interests: in the mortal and the angel the temporal and the eternal meet, and in their union lies 'Christ's promise to man of a release from time (*CP*, 223). Similarly "The Christmas" is to Muir "The marriage feast of heaven and earth" when "An infant's cry across the snow / Rouses the never-setting day." As usual Muir associates the specific Christian event with other religions and so, through references to the winter solstice, he treats the birth of Christ as a ritual rebirth: "The menial earth / . . . strews with emblems of rebirth / The burial of the solar year" (*OFE*, 38). "The Son" focuses on the suffering of Christ in his mortal body; the poem is indeed "quite inadequate," largely because of its form, the same short-lined, rhymed quatrain which caused many of Muir's earlier failures.

"The Killing" is the most striking poem in the group. It is a dramatic soliloquy in blank verse in which "a stranger" (perhaps the same Greek merchant of the "Soliloquy" in *The Labyrinth*) who could "not read these people / Or this outlandish deity" describes the Good Friday scene:

> We watched the writhings, heard the moanings, saw
> The three heads turning on their separate axles
> Like broken wheels left spinning. Round *his* head

> Was loosely bound a crown of plaited thorn
> That hurt at random, stinging temple and brow
> As the pain swung into its envious circle.
>
> (*CP*, 224)

He watches the spectators who had "prayed for a Rabbi or an armed Messiah / And found the Son of God" and wonders, "Did a God / Indeed in dying cross my life that day / By chance, he on his road and I on mine?" Although Muir never attempted to compose a drama, his soliloquies are among his strongest poems and reveal in their technique his dramatic awareness. In "The Killing" the details that centuries of pietistic verse have made familiar are given new scope because they are seen through the eyes of a "stranger" who is willing to accept the crucified man as "a God."

The religious significance of these poems is summed up in the last lines of "Lost and Found." Since that moment in time that God took upon himself mortal flesh, all men are "Sons, daughters, brothers, sisters of that Prince / . . . by grace, although in banishment" (*OFE*, 43). Between this sonnet and the other affirmative sonnet, "The Lord," is interposed "Antichrist," an ingenious argument in which Muir admits that every positive thing implies its negative, and thus for Christ there must be an anti-Christ. Yet his presence is not the truth, for "He is the Lie; one true thought, and he's gone" (*CP*, 226). Further affirmation is given in "The Lord": the poet writes that he would suffer any fate rather

> Than be with those, the clever and the dull,
> Who say that lord is dead; when I can hear
> Daily his dying whisper in my ear.
>
> (*OFE*, 45)

The last two poems in this group are important statements of the poet's mature religious faith. The title poem of the collection demonstrates the joyful acceptance of the world in which man must live: this acceptance accounts for much of the calm beauty of this and other of the late poems.[18] Here in these "fields of charity and sin / Where we shall lead our harvest in" stand "Evil and good," for "nothing now can separate / The corn and tares compactly grown." And accepting this world, the poet realizes that out of the "terror and grief" and from the "famished field and blackened tree" come "flowers in Eden never known."

Blossoms of grief and charity
Bloom in these darkened fields alone.
What had Eden ever to say
Of hope and faith and pity and love
Until was buried all its day
And memory found its treasure trove?
Strange blessings never in Paradise
Fall from these beclouded skies.

(*CP*, 227)

Again Muir uses the idea of the "fortunate fall," adding to it the logical extension that the Christian virtues are also part of the "strange blessings" following upon the expulsion from the Garden. Thus his acceptance of this world of sin has a place within his Christian attitude.

There is a sort of pawky humor in the fact that this poem, based on a traditional doctrine developed by theologians, is followed by "The Incarnate One," an attack on organized religion ("King Calvin with his iron pen") and on theologians who would "betray / The Image" and "unmake . . . the Incarnate One" so that "The Word made flesh here is made word again." The poem goes far to explain not only why Muir never turned to any of the Christian churches after he acknowledged his Christian faith but also why these last volumes are so eclectic in their religious attitudes. Muir instinctively turned away from any expression of belief touched by orthodoxy, anything that might cause "the Mystery [to be] impaled and bent / Into an ideological instrument." Always, to the poet, "There's better gospel in man's natural tongue." The poem ends with his affirmation of the worth of the individual, for in him the "bloodless word will battle for its own / Invisibly in brain and nerve and cell"; and in the individual "the One has far to go / Past the mirages and the murdering snow" (*CP*, 228 - 29).

The references to the "murdering snow" and to the plight of Christianity in Scotland allow Muir to include here the poem he wrote in the mid-1930s for his travel book *Scottish Journey*.[19] "Scotland's Winter" describes a land where past glories are buried and the poeple "are content / With their poor frozen life and shallow banishment" (*CP*, 229). This characteristically mid-1930s attitude is heard again in the first of the two sonnets which bring this section to a close. "The Great House" is a highly allegorical poem, the main idea being that there is a "due time" when "order" must come "to disorder." Even while accepting the inevitable changes of life, the poet can write, "Praise the few / Who built in chaos our bastion and our home" (*CP*, 230). This joyful realization of man's inheritance—the "bastion" that the memory of Eden provides—brings Muir to the final sonnet, "The Emblem." Fredrick Garber, studying "Edwin Muir's Heraldic Mode," sensibly treats this poem as yet another description of "the realm, apparently dried up in the blasts of time, that runs parallel to our daily round; . . . within the realm . . . all are found in their proper positions in a hierarchy that Muir never defines in more detail than this."[20] The clue to the meaning of the poem lies in the phrase "this [place] will seem a little tangled field": the present world offers little comparison to the archetypal world of Eden which the poet can always remember. This world of innocence is referred to by "The six-inch king and the toy treasury," toys of childhood suggestive of its wealth. Yet in case the poet should be accused of constantly looking back to some make-believe, "good old times," he asserts, "I am not, although I seem, an antiquary, / For that scant-acre kingdom is not dead, / Nor save in seeming shrunk" (*CP*, 230 - 31). Having taken the reader of this first half of the collection through man's history, never failing to acknowledge the doubts and fears that inevitably accompany such a journey, the poet remains secure in his belief, restated in this final sonnet, that "Paradise" lies all about man, who need take only "A footstep more" in order to see "far and near the fields of Paradise" (*CP*, 207).

B. *Part Two*

The poems in the second part are less tightly arranged than those in the first part, although Muir follows a certain logic. Again a sonnet provides the introduction and states the general theme. "To Franz Kafka" is both a graceful appreciation of the author whom Muir had so long championed and a critical evaluation of Kafka. It also suggests the nature of the following poems. Framed in theological terms, it suggests that "we, the proximate damned, presumptive blest," who hardly know ourselves and "ignore" the way we should live, are actually insignificant beside "the authentic ones, the worst and best / Picked from all time." But Kafka, who was the "sad champion of the drab / And half," could see in our lives and stories of "tell-tale shames" the "secret script" of eternity, which is "the saving proof" (*CP*, 233). The poem declares the worth of the individual and praises the artist who can discern that worth.

In the following poems Muir looks at different human beings and situations and tries himself to find the "secret script" in them. Yet just as Kafka's undeniably human characters and situations often seem paradoxically devoid of humanity, so do Muir's poems here frequently give the impression of enigmatic abstractions. The key to the enigma lies in remembering Muir's belief that Kafka's novels and stories are narrative inventions which express "a general or universal situation."[21] If one looks behind the poems for those universal qualities, one soon realizes that the often difficult language frequently cloaks fairly simple ideas.

Such an approach works well for the five-part poem "Effigies." Descriptions of five individuals (or character types), the effigies reveal that visions of Eden-Paradise did not prevent Muir from seeing the evil about him and the harsh reality faced by man in his daily life. The first poem concerns the man who controls all things, to the eventual destruction of his own happiness (CP, 233). Peter Butter calls it "the most unsparing portrait of an evil man that [Muir] ever drew."[22] In the second poem Muir suggests that the betrayer is to be pitied since the man whom he betrays finds freedom in his death ("The envied and beloved quarry fled / Long since for death and freedom"); but the betrayer is caught in the trap he has constructed and cannot release himself (CP, 234). The third poem centers on the idea that when man cuts himself off from other men "to be with himself alone," his life becomes meaningless (CP, 235). More characteristic themes are given in the fourth and fifth poems, Muir once more declaring that the dead assert their reality through their constant presence before the living. In the last poem, he stresses that to live out of touch with the sensuous world—to live in the "echo" of the song, not in the "aria" itself—is to reap a reward of no value (CP, 236).

These negative ideas about mankind are immediately contradicted in the following poem, "The Difficult Land." Certainly, Muir writes, this world "is a difficult land," since "Here things miscarry / Whether we care, or do not care enough." The examples he presents of the difficulties of farming and of the invasions of foreign armies might come from the life of some medieval peasant; and they effectively give the lie to the accusation that Muir's sense of the ordered past, that idea which figures so largely in his critical writings, is a romantic notion divorced from reality. But in spite of these difficulties, Muir knows that man is sustained by "faces of goodness, faithful masks of sorrow, / Honesty, kindness, courage, fidelity, / The love that lasts a life's time." The evil described in

"Effigies" exists, but it is overcome by good. To the casual reader
this good may appear to be detached from religious considerations,
but the lines "For how can we reject / The long last look on the
ever-dying face / Turned backward from the other side of time"
must be a reference to Christ, since it is He alone who links the eternal ("the other side of time") and the temporal. Man cannot turn
his back upon this world, for it was in this world that Christ's never-
ceasing sacrifice was made for man. "This is a difficult country,"
Muir concludes, "and our home" (*CP*, 237 - 38).

Again like the resolution of some difficult harmony a sonnet
appears in the order of poems to reiterate the idea already
suggested, that in this world there is "Nothing there but faith" (*CP*,
238 - 39). This affirmation is repeated in "Double Absence," a
statement of the beauty of this world, which, although obviously
stemming from a personal experience (the sight of a singing thrush
in a tree), is nevertheless not unrelated in subject matter and tone to
Thomas Hardy's lyric "The Darkling Thrush." Even in these late
poems there are occasional instances when Muir's language and
symbols remain impenetrable, as they do in "Double Absence"
(*CP*, 239). But such poems are more than outweighed by those in
which the private experience is expressed in language so simple that
it is open to all readers and is yet so rich that its meanings continue
to expand with each reading. "Day and Night" deserves such
praise. Again it is a consideration of the "story" and the "fable,"
and again Muir points to the unconscious and the dream life as a
source of the "fable":

> The night, the night alone is old
> And showed me only what I knew,
> Knew, yet never had been told;
> A speech that from the darkness grew
> Too deep for daily tongues to say,
> Archaic dialogue of a few
> Upon the sixth or the seventh day.
> (*CP*, 240)

The poet wants to hold the "hidden" and the "visible" worlds side
by side, for both are needed by man. The poem ends with the
familiar journey image, which here finds one of its most felicitous
expressions. The poet desires to

> Learn from the shepherd of the dark,
> Here in the light, the paths to know
> That thread the labyrinthine park,

> And the great Roman roads that go
> Striding across the untrodden day.
>   (*CP*, 240)

The richness of these metaphors, achieved through the terms of the personification ("roads . . . Striding . . . untrodden") and through the combination of images (the night road carrying man through the new day), amply demonstrates the achievement of Edwin Muir in these late poems.

And yet the ideas in these poems are almost always those which Muir expresses in earlier poems. "The Other Story" has to do with memories of man's primal innocence and of his "Revolt or sin or guilt or shame"—they are what is meant by *original sin*, "the sad memorial name / First uttered by the offence" (*CP*, 241). Similarly "Dream and Thing" places the "hidden" and "visible" worlds side by side, stressing the need to "bring / From the dull mass each separate splendour out" (*CP*, 242). This emphasis on individuality as opposed to collectivism (in Muir an idea stemming from his political convictions, but also one of the most characteristic features of modern British poetry) also appears in "Song for a Hypothetical Age": in it the poet sardonically writes that in "our new impersonal age . . . dry is every eye" while "The last grief is passing by." Once more using the constancy of Penelope as his example, Muir declares that when heart and earth are turned to stone, then "Grief and joy no more shall wake." The mature poet knows that the promise of "inevitable . . . happiness" held out by political systems and philosophical creeds which would shape a new age is false because it denies the real world in which man must live—a world in which the acceptance of grief makes possible the development of joy (*CP*, 242 - 43). A similar message is found in "The Young Princes," where the dispossessed princes, the rightful heirs of the kingdom, have suffered the "Doubt that kills courtesy and gratitude," but can still "Know what we are, remembering what we were" (*CP*, 244). In "The Cloud" Muir remembers the farmworker he saw harrowing a field in Communist Czechoslovakia and walking over the earth in a cloud of dust: the poet longs "for light to break / And show that his face was the face once broken in Eden / . . . / And not a blindfold mask on a pillar of dust" (*CP*, 245 - 46). Both poems succeed because the metaphors adequately convey Muir's familiar message.

While the ideas remain constant in these late poems, Muir shows his awareness of the contemporary scene in his choice of subjects, metaphors, and language. The preceding three poems reflect the political situation that developed in Czechoslovakia while Muir was there and the twentieth-century acceptance of collectivism as opposed to individualism. The post-Hiroshima world with its concept of nuclear holocaust stands behind the evocative poem "The Horses," a fusion of images that had haunted Muir throughout his life with the Zeitgeist of the 1950s. Muir describes the world after "The seven days war that put the world to sleep": all mechanical things have stopped, and there is no communication or transportation; life surprisingly continues, but mankind has had to return to the soil as the source of the necessities of life, and this return to the agrarian life has brought with it a sense of order and stability (*CP*, 246). Man resolves to manage without the tractors and to live in a new relationship with the world of nature. At this point "the strange horses" appear, bringing with them "some half-a-dozen colts / Dropped in some wilderness of the broken world." The speakers are afraid, for they do not understand the relationship between man and beast; but the horses "waited,"

> Stubborn and shy, as if they had been sent
> By an old command to find our whereabouts
> And that long-lost archaic companionship.
> (*CP*, 247)

Men and beasts come together in a new relationship in which each has a vital part, and in which each freely gives what he has to give:

> Since then they have pulled our ploughs and borne our loads,
> But that free servitude still can pierce our hearts.
> Our life is changed; their coming our beginning.
> (*CP*, 247)

The central image is similar to that in the poem about horses in the *First Poems*;[23] but whereas in the 1920s the animal stood for itself and, perhaps, for a sense of the mystery of an alien life, here the horses represent all aspects of the natural life, a life close to, if not the same as, that of the archetypal world. It is characteristic of Muir that in dealing with a subject—nuclear holocaust—that in most writers usually brings out their pessimism, he is able to see in disaster the potential of a change for good and to look forward to good rather than to evil.

In "The Horses" Muir writes of a return to an archetypal world, and in the three following poems he treats other aspects of this idea.

The "Song," based on the myth of Persephone, achieves originality
by the use of an unfamiliar point of view: the underworld mourns
the resurrection of Persephone and rejoices at her death, for she en-
joys a "strange twofold immortality" (CP, 248). This myth leads on
to "The Island," a hymn of praise for the continuity of the
archetypal life which Muir saw when he visited Sicily. The world
which understood the change of the seasons as the death and
resurrection of Persephone continues its life here on the Mediterra-
nean island, the natural world speaking "through the transmuted
tongue" (CP, 248 - 49). This unity of the quick and the dead is the
subject also of "Into Thirty Centuries Born," in which Muir maintains that man is at home in time, except for the present century,
and that "We meet ourselves at every turn / In the long country of
the past" (CP, 249 - 51). The poem is akin to those about time in
Journeys and Places, and like them its abstractions often deny the
communication of thought. This section is brought to a close by the
sonnet "My Own," a statement that there is no reason why man
should turn away from his true path through life (CP, 251 - 52).

One Foot in Eden is concluded by five lyrics, "The Choice," "If I
Could Know," "The Late Wasp," "The Late Swallow," and
"Song" (CP, 252 - 54). The common themes are the acceptance of
the journey through life into death, and a celebration of the love
that makes man's life creative and meaningful. The companion
poems in this group, "The Late Wasp" and "The Late Swallow"
(CP, 253), offer interesting examples of Muir's practice in handling
symbols. Muir describes the wasp which must soon die in the cold
air; and he tells the swallow that it must migrate to a more
hospitable climate. To understand Muir's intentions the reader
must take insect and bird to be insect and bird, and must accept the
limitations which their natures put upon them—the insect lives for
one season, the bird must migrate in order to live. In this acceptance the reader thus practices a principle (that of acceptance itself)
without which no one can live joyfully in the temporal world. But
the significance does not stop with this reaction to the laws of
nature: the wasp, because it must live in its limited time, must die
in time, while the swallow, which can preserve its life over a longer
span, can make the journey that will bring it to a place of refuge,
"the radiant tree" where the bird can "light and perch." The
further meaning develops from the cultural significance of the insect as having a limited life span and from the ancient metaphor
comparing man's soul to a bird which, flying into life as into a

lighted room, must at death fly back into the darkness from which it came. The two poems contrast the life lived solely in the phenomenal world and in its pleasures (the wasp has "fed on the marmalade / So deeply, all your strength was scarcely able / To prise you from the sweet pit you had made") with the life lived in companionship with others of one's kind and with whom one must journey toward a meaningful, indeed inevitable, destination. The poems are yet further extensions of the journey-of-life theme in which the poet asserts the value and meaningfulness of the journey man must take.

It would be wrong to examine the poems in *The Labyrinth* and *One Foot in Eden* as the work of a philosopher who attempted to formulate a rational system of thought, for Edwin Muir was always a poet who relied on his intuitive knowledge. Yet a consistent belief emerges from his poems which accounts for their fundamental value and importance. The basis of this belief is a faith in the worth and meaning of the individual human life, life which begins before the earthly years and which continues after death. This belief is in-, timately involved with Christianity, although it is not by any definition an orthodox Christian faith. *One Foot in Eden* shows that Edwin Muir was essentially a religious poet who only in his last years defined and controlled his understanding of human life so that he could express in poetry that vision which transcends the temporal. Like his Milton, Edwin Muir also saw with "unblinded eyes . . . the fields of Paradise."

III   *"Poems Not Previously Collected,"* Collected Poems *(1960)*

In summer 1956 Willa and Edwin returned from the United States with enough money to buy a house, and in the Cambridgeshire village of Swaffham Prior, some eight miles outside Cambridge, they found Priory Cottage, three old cottages joined together to form one comfortable house. Here Muir continued to write the reviews which supported them and to compose a steady flow of poems. It was from Priory Cottage that he wrote to T. S. Eliot about a proposed new edition of his *Collected Poems*, the first edition having initially appeared in 1953 under the editorship of John C. Hall, a London poet and journalist who had suggested to Muir the idea of such a collection and who found, somewhat to his surprise, Muir asking him to be the editor. Eliot "suggested that *One Foot in Eden* should be included, but probably not new poems written since then if there was a prospect of there soon being enough for a new volume."[24] But Muir's health grew worse in the autumn and plans for the new edition were delayed; and when Muir died in January 1959 Mrs. Muir, Eliot, and Hall agreed to include as a final section in the *Collected Poems* the "Poems Not Previously Collected." These are in three groups: those published in periodicals or sent to editors in a final form; those obviously not completed; and those in a fragmentary state. This section clearly reveals in its unpolished presentation the care Muir exercised in putting his collections together and suggests that the revisions in his poems were made with the intention of fitting them into a harmonious whole. These poems lack the overall unity of *The Labyrinth* and *One Foot in Eden* and show the unguarded image of the poet. Individual poems do not contradict the ideas of earlier ones; but they distort the proportions and alter the play of light and dark which Muir so carefully contrived through his sequence of arrangement.

These poems do not, like those in the two previous collections, project the image of the whole man, although their topics indicate Muir's interests in his last years. For the most part they concern subjects handled in previous poems—religious faith, classical myths, the poet's relationship with his past, including long-dead family members—and topics emerging from his life from 1956 to 1958, particularly his experiences in the United States in 1956 - 1957. In those poems in which Muir treats both his lifelong concerns and his new experiences one sees the vitality and artistry which inform the best of these late poems. "The Church" is representative. During their stay at Harvard, as Willa Muir remembered, she and Edwin could see from their hotel room "a new church being built . . . day by day it grew, until one day the skeleton of its spire was set up, delicately pencilled against the autumn sky with a small gilt cross on top."[25] Looking at this ancient symbol erected in the New World, Muir felt an ancestral connection:

> Someone inside me sketches a cross—askew,
> A child's—on seeing that stick crossed with a stick,
> Some simple ancestor, perhaps, that knew,
> Centuries ago when all were Catholic,
> That this archaic trick
> Brings to the heart and the fingers what was done
> One spring day in Judaea to Three in One[.]
>   (*CP*, 263)

Recognizing such eternal mysteries, the poet is not misled by the opulence of the physical building or by the complexities invented by "ingenious theological men" who "crib in rusty bars / The Love that moves the sun and the other stars." Nor does it matter, he implies, that all life is so different in this foreign country where the church finds a multitude of forms, and nothing appears to be finished. "I look," he writes, "and do not doubt that He is there" (*CP*, 264). Typical of these late poems, "The Church" makes an unqualified statement of belief, free from any qualifications.

Muir was forcibly affected by the strangeness of American life; indeed Willa Muir remarks of their reaction, "We had had to come to America to find how European we were."[26] Thus although some poems, like "Salem, Massachusetts," reveal Muir's explicit reaction to American life and history (*CP*, 264), others show rather his withdrawal into his own resources. His sense of alienation caused him either to ponder such contemporary ideas about the future as are expressed in "After 1984" (*CP*, 267 - 68) and "The Last War" (*CP*, 282 - 85), or to write about his psychic experiences with renewed faith in their validity. The "futuristic" poems are not unlike those in earlier collections, for although Muir's realization of the possibilities of evil in this world grew stronger with age, his faith in an ultimate goal for man remained unshaken. In the "Dialogue" he says to his interlocutor, "This is not the end of the world's road," and then, changing the image, calls man's life on earth "A house, and there we nourish a heavenly hope." His religious faith is the basis for his "hope": "For this a great god died and all heaven mourned / That earth might, in extremity, have such fortune" (*CP*, 275). This unqualified faith is also expressed in the "Sonnet," which begins, "You will not leave us, for You cannot, Lord."

The poems which originate in Muir's psychic experiences—even those which were never completed—are often the most satisfying among these last poems. The cause is not far to seek: Muir's life experiences had confirmed his intuitive belief, and in these poems he makes no apologies or explanations: the experience *is*. The fragment "I see the image" indicates this quality (*CP*, 297), but of these last poems "The Brothers" best represents Muir's characteristic themes. In a low-keyed yet inevitable rhetoric, he describes a dream he had had of his brothers playing "In a field two yards away," although "For half a century they were gone / . . . / To be among the peaceful dead." The strife and disorder which he had seen in their earthly lives and in their deaths (and which he had written about in both *The Three Brothers* and *Poor Tom*) have completely disappeared, and he wonders, "How could I be so dull, / Twenty thousand days ago, / Not to see they were beautiful?"(*CP*, 272). In life, man's first form, that form shown in the Transfiguration, is covered by "A darkness . . . [and] / Frowns twisted the original face," and the earthly body hides "The beauty and the buried grace." In the last stanza Muir gives a summary of his basic faith, explaining that his visionary life described in the poem compensates for the injustices of earthly life:

> I have observed in foolish awe
> The dateless mid-days of the law
> And seen indifferent justice done
> By everyone on everyone.
> And in a vision I have seen
> My brothers playing on the green.
>
>   (*CP*, 273)

As Muir writes in the fragment, "I have been taught," which fittingly brings this section to a close, "dreams and fantasies" given to him by the hosts of the dead and particularly "from two mainly / Who gave me birth" have given him direction through life, so that

> . . . now the time grows shorter, I perceive
> That Plato's is the truest poetry,
> And that these shadows
> Are cast by the true.
>
>   (*CP*, 302)

IV   *Conclusion*

To assess the literary achievement of Edwin Muir, whose career encompassed so many different literary roles, one must consider separately each genre in which he wrote, for inevitably he was more successful in some areas than in others. In spite of this uneven accomplishment, his ability to write within so many different forms must be considered one of Muir's assets. Indeed Edwin Muir was a "man of letters" in the traditional sense of the term, and he can profitably be compared to similar figures in earlier periods, men like Charles Cowden Clarke, W. M. Rossetti, and William Archer, who are rarely remembered today save by the literary historian, even though in their lifetime they were better known than those writers whom time has proved to be more important. In this light Muir appears as a purveyor of literature to the larger reading public. He was not (like many men of letters) an editor, but rather the actual writer, whose standards and ideas inevitably helped in their wide dissemination to shape the literary consciousness of at least two generations of English readers. To the literary historian and particularly the student of popular taste Edwin Muir will be remembered as an important figure on the English literary scene for some four decades.

But this general assessment does not reveal the measure of Muir's artistic accomplishment, which appears only from an examination of his actual writings in the different genres. His work as a general writer of biography, travel literature, political essays, and whatever else he was assigned by an editor or publisher reveals his competence to produce books and essays that satisfied many discriminating readers. His biography of Knox is an appropriate example of this sort of writing. A commissioned book, written from research in an area in which the author had no particular training, it was accepted both by the general reader and by specialized historians, largely because Muir was an interesting writer who could impart his individual point of view and color his narrative by his own pleasing personality. In short, Edwin Muir the man made a success of Edwin Muir the professional writer.

The translations also belong to the "general writer," and, in addition, they resulted as much from Willa Muir's efforts as from Edwin's. But the lives of the husband and the wife were so closely interwoven that no assessment of Edwin can avoid mention of Willa. These translations fall into two groups, those novels which were originally written and then translated in the hopes that they might become best-sellers (Feuchtwanger's *Jew Süss* is one that succeeded in this aim), and those novels in which the author attempted to create a work of art (Kafka's and Broch's novels are the obvious examples). The Muirs' success with the former group is indicated by the number of novels they were commissioned to translate, while the widespread acceptance of Kafka and the growing knowledge of Broch among the English-reading public prove the importance of the Muirs' work. The translations of Kafka have been revised by later translators (as was perhaps inevitable for such a difficult writer) but the Muirs must always be given credit for introducing Kafka to the British and American publics.

Turning to Muir's work as a literary critic one moves closer to

Muir the man. Having no specialized training in language or literature to fall back on, and owing no allegiance to any literary clique or movement, Muir relied solely on his intuitive response and native intelligence when he discussed literature. His personal sensitivity to the effect which criticism has upon a writer caused him not to be less outspoken or honest than he might have been, but rather to shape his evaluation in such a way that it might be helpful to the writer under discussion. This attitude involves Muir in the creative writer's ongoing work and gives even his journalistic work—the book reviews which he wrote with such regularity and his essays on avant-garde literature for popular journals—a vitality that is not often found in such work. Incidentally there is considerable evidence that contemporary writers appreciated Muir's aims, if not his critical comments; to give only one example, Muir's essay on Eliot in August 1925 resulted in a letter from Eliot in which (according to Muir) Eliot " 'thought [the essay] very good, disagreed with it, but said it had been useful to him. In short, it was an astonishingly nice letter. . . .' "[27] Throughout his life Muir saw his critical work as a dialogue with the writer rather than as an evaluation for the reader. This attitude helped to keep him in touch with contemporary movements in literature and to give him a catholic understanding of his own and younger generations.

When Muir turned to more purely speculative criticism, he brought his intuitive ideas into play and created (I refer specifically to *The Structure of the Novel* and some of the essays in *Essays on Literature and Society*) original work that students of literature continue to find helpful. These writings are distinguished by their fresh approach, by their reflection of the winning personality of the author, and by the overall feeling in them that literature is a valuable and meaningful record of human experience. Certainly these are not the hallmarks of a new critical stance, and Edwin Muir will never be credited with originating a new critical approach to literature. On the other hand, his thoughtful, sympathetic appreciations which always focus upon the work of literature—rather than upon the critical apparatus—are similar to nineteenth-century essays which are still read today; and Muir's failure to develop idiosyncratic critical standards may cause his essays to be sought out by readers when the more original critics of his day are remembered only by literary historians.

Muir rises above any estimate made of him as a man of letters or literary critic when he is considered as an imaginative writer. The novels, autobiographies, and poems all proceed from the same source. To define it would be to define Edwin Muir the man, and one must fall back on psychological terms of description and on comparisons with other poets. These works spring from Muir's Wordsworthian response to himself. That is, like the author of *The Prelude* he too finds in his intuitive response to life, in his subconscious life of dreams and fantasy, and in his recognition of the eternal archetypes the meaning and justification of his own existence and of human life. But Muir's response is also informed by the teachings of twentieth-century psychology which give him a sharper, more precise vision of this age-old wisdom, and by his faith in Christ as the manifestation of the Godhead. Surprisingly, in the light of his involvement with contemporary literature and his avowed role as promoter of new writing, his verse shows few signs of the age in which it was written, either in technique or presentation. In the light of its content, however, this quality is not altogether surprising, for Muir instinctively knew that his traditional ideas precluded any presentation that was colored by one specific age. The truth and wisdom in these poems are limited only by the span of human life on this earth, not by the poet's limited life span.

For the first years of his writing career Muir was best known as a critic and translator, and the reception of his poems was influenced by his reputation as a professional writer. Gradually, during the 1940s and 1950s, his poems came to be evaluated in their own right; and today, with the fading away of his name as an essayist and translator, he is known primarily as a poet. The type of poems which he wrote, embodying the traditional wisdom of civilized man and relying upon the reader's grasp of various religious and psychological concepts, will probably never be as widely read as Yeats's or even Robert Graves's poems because Muir demands such an intense response from the reader. And Muir's refusal to hold to one attitude to life and hence to become a spokesman for one particular group cuts him off from supporters like those of Eliot's verse. The poems Muir wrote link him with those traditional poets like Vaughan, Blake, and Wordsworth. Their appeal has always been to the serious thinker, and their value, even in periods when they have not been widely read, has never been questioned. Though restricted in output and in range of themes, and limited in terms of influence, Edwin Muir holds a definite place in the succession of these traditional poets and must be ranked among the most important of the twentieth-century British poets.

Notes and References

Chapter One

1. Biographical information is taken from Edwin Muir, *The Story and the Fable* (London, 1940) and from the expanded revision, *An Autobiography* (London, New York, 1954); from Peter H. Butter, *Edwin Muir: Man and Poet* (Edinburgh, 1966); Peter H. Butter, ed., *Selected Letters of Edwin Muir* (London, 1974); Willa Muir, *Belonging: A Memoir* (London, 1968); and from private sources.

2. For information about the *New Age* and Muir's relationship to it, see Wallace Martin, *The New Age under Orage: Chapters in English Cultural History* (Manchester, New York, 1967).

3. "Obituary," *Times* (London), 5 Jan. 1959, p. 10.

4. P. 154.

5. The psychologist was identified as Maurice Nicoll by Michael Hamburger in his essay "Edwin Muir," *Encounter*, 15 (Dec. 1960), 47. Additional information about Nicoll is given by Beryl Pogson, *Maurice Nicoll* (London, 1961).

6. *Athenaeum*, 28 Jan. 1921, pp. 90 - 91; reprinted Edwin Muir, *Latitudes* (London, 1924), pp. 94 - 102.

7. H. L. Mencken, "Introduction," Edwin Muir, *We Moderns: Enigmas and Guesses* (New York, 1920), p. 20.

8. *An Autobiography*, p. 246. The original diary entry, much longer than that in *An Autobiography*, is quoted by Peter Butter, *Edwin Muir: Man and Poet*, pp. 167 - 69.

9. *An Autobiography*, p. 247.

10. Ibid., p. 278.

Chapter Two

1. (London), p. 132.

2. "Fiction," *Nation*, 37 (30 May 1925), 270.

3. "Fiction," *Nation*, 38 (20 Feb. 1926), 719.

4. "Recent Criticism," *Nation*, 36 (6 Dec. 1924), 370.

5. "Herman Melville," *Nation*, 39 (19 June 1926), 324; "Maupassant," *Nation*, 39 (18 Sept. 1926), 704; "A Study of Swinburne," *Nation*, 40 (11 Dec. 1926), 390.

6. "Henry James," *Nation*, 40 (1 Jan. 1927), 483.

7. "New Novels," *Listener*, 10 (23 Aug. 1933), 294.

8. "New Novels," *Listener*, 16 (5 Aug. 1936), 278.

9. "New Novels," *Listener*, 20 (21 July 1938), 153.

10. "New Novels," *Listener*, 22 (28 Sept. 1939), 638.

11. "New Novels," *Listener*, 12 (19 Sept. 1934), 506.

12. "New Novels," *Listener*, 29 (4 Feb. 1943), 154.

13. *Transition* (London), pp. 101 - 13. The essay was first published in the *Nation* (New York), 122 (10 Feb. 1926), 144 - 45.

14. "New Novels," *Listener*, 16 (8 July 1936), 92.

15. "New Novels," *Listener*, 11 (4 April 1934), 596.

16. "James Joyce's New Novel," *Listener*, 21 (11 May 1939), 1013.

17. Q. D. Leavis, "The Literary Life Respectable" [review of *The Story and the Fable*], *Scrutiny*, 9 (Sept. 1940), 171.

18. Virginia Woolf, *A Writer's Diary* (London, 1953), p. 280; Edwin Muir, "New Novels," *Listener*, 17 (31 March 1937), 622.

19. J. B. Priestley, *Margin Released: A Writer's Reminiscences and Reflections* (New York, 1962), p. 193; Edwin Muir, "New Novels," *Listener*, 30 (29 July 1943), 134.

20. *London Magazine*, 3 (Jan. 1956), 51 - 52; Edwin Muir, "New Novels," *Listener*, 10 (8 Nov. 1933), 728.

21. "Translation of Poetry," *Scotsman*, 14 May 1936, p. 15; "Rilke Translated," *Scotsman*, 23 Nov. 1936, p. 15; "A French Poet's World," *Scotsman*, 29 Oct. 1936, p. 15.

22. "De Quincey's Genius," *Scotsman*, 27 April 1936, p. 13; "An Urbane Realist," *Scotsman*, 26 March 1936, p. 6.

23. "Mr. Eliot's New Play," *Scotsman*, 23 March 1939, p. 6; "From Donne to Keats," *Scotsman*, 15 Oct. 1936, p. 15; "Odious Comparisons," *Scotsman*, 7 March 1935, p. 15.

24. As in his review of Brooks's *The Well-Wrought Urn:* "Poetic Method," *Observer*, 11 Sept. 1949, p. 7.

25. "The Poor Critic," *Observer*, 1 May 1955, p. 17. Muir paraphrases this review in *The Estate of Poetry* (Cambridge, Mass., 1962), pp. 73 - 75.

26. Edwin Muir, *John Knox: Portrait of a Calvinist* (London, 1929), p. ix. References in the text labeled *JK* are to this volume.

27. *An Autobiography* (London, 1954), p. 231.

28. Edwin Muir, *Scottish Journey* (London, 1935), p. 46. References in the text labeled *SJ* are to this volume.

29. Edwin Muir, *Social Credit and the Labour Party, An Appeal* (London, 1935), p. 15. References in the text labeled *SC* are to this pamphlet.

30. (London), pp. 128.

31. (London), pp. 32.

32. The quotation is from a letter to the present writer in 1961 by Willa Muir, who used almost the same terms in *Belonging* (London, 1968), p. 150.

33. Kurt Heuser, *Inner Journey* (1932; American title, *Journey Inward*); Ernst Lothar, *Little Friend* (1933) and *The Mills of God* (1935); Heinrich Mann, *Hill of Lies* (1934).

34. Sholem Asch, *Three Cities* (1933), *Salvation* (1934), *Mottke the Thief* (1935), and *Calf of Paper* (1936; American title, *War Goes On*).

35. Emil Rheinhardt, *The Life of Eleanora Duse* (1930); Georges Paléologue, *Enigmatic Czar* (1938); and Carl Burckhardt, *Richelieu* (1940); Zsolt Harsányi, *Lover of Life* (1942); and Robert Neumann, *The Queen's Doctor* (1936).

36. The other two translations were of *The Child Manuela* (1933) and *Life Begins* (1935), both by C. Winsloe, Baroness Hatvany.

37. "A Note on Hans Carossa," *Bookman*, 72 (Dec. 1930), 405 - 406.

38. "Some Letters of Edwin Muir," *Encounter*, 26 (Jan. 1966), 8; reprinted in *Selected Letters of Edwin Muir*, ed. Peter H. Butter (London, 1974), p. 69.

39. "Translating from the German," in Reuben A. Brower, ed., *On Translation* (Cambridge, Mass., 1959), p. 94.

40. Hermann Broch, *Briefe von 1929 bis 1951*, Ges. *Werke*, Bd. 8, ed. Robert Pick (Zurich, 1957), pp. 50 - 51.

41. "Hermann Broch," *Bookman*, 75 (Nov. 1932), 666.

42. Thomas Koebner, *Hermann Broch* (Bern, 1965), p. 74.

43. See below, pp. 112 - 14.

44. *Times Literary Supplement*, 31 May 1963, p. 389.

45. (Frankfurt am Main), p. 436 (translated from the German).

46. "Introductory Note," Franz Kafka, *The Castle*, translated by Edwin and Willa Muir (New York, 1930), p. vii. In italics in the original.

47. Ibid., pp. vii - viii.

48. Ibid., p. x.

49. In *Six Poems* (Warlingham, Surrey), pp. 7 - 8.

50. "Introductory Note," Franz Kafka, *The Great Wall of China, and Other Pieces*, translated by Edwin and Willa Muir (London, 1933), p. xiii.

51. Max Brod, *Franz Kafka, eine Biographie* (Prague).

52. "Introductory Note," Franz Kafka, *America*, translated by Edwin and Willa Muir (London, 1938), p. xi.

53. Ibid., p. viii.

54. "From Kafka's Diaries: Excerpts," *New Statesman*, 21 (29 March 1941), 321 - 22; *Saturday Review of Literature*, 24 (26 July 1941), 3 - 4.

55. Edwin Muir, "Franz Kafka" in *A Franz Kafka Miscellany* (New York, 1940), p. 60. References in the text labeled *FKM* are to this volume.

56. "Poznámka k Franzi Kafkovi," *Franz Kafka a Praha* (Prague, 1947); "Franz Kafka," *Essays on Literature and Society* (London, 1949; Cambridge, Mass., 1965), pp. 120 - 24 (American edn.). References in the text labeled *ELS* are to the American edition.

57. This quotation comes from the last paragraph of the essay in the 1949 edition; the paragraph is omitted in the 1965 edition.

58. *Critical Quarterly*, 6 (1964), 231.

Chapter Three

1. "Edwin Muir," *Encounter*, 15 (Dec. 1960), 49.

2. *Latitudes* (London, New York, 1924), pp. 85, 86. References in the text labeled *L* are to the American edition.

3. *Transition, Essays on Contemporary Literature* (London, New York), pp. 4 - 5. References in the text labeled *T* are to the American edition.

4. "James Joyce: The Meaning of 'Ulysses'," 1 (July 1925), 347 - 55.

5. "A Note on *Ulysses*," 41 (10 Dec. 1924 [Supplement]), 4 - 6.

6. "Some Letters of Edwin Muir," *Encounter*, 26 (Jan. 1966), 6.

7. *The Structure of the Novel* (London, 1928; New York, 1929), p. 17. References in the text labeled *SN* are to the American edition.

8. *The European Quarterly*, No. 1 (May 1934), p. 2.

9. A survey of this movement will be found in Kurt Wittig, *The Scottish Tradition in Literature* (Edinburgh, 1958), Chapter 10. See also Duncan Glen, *Hugh MacDiarmid (Christopher Murray Grieve) and the Scottish Renaissance* (Edinburgh, 1964).

10. "Literature from 1910 to 1935," 4 May 1935, p. xiii.

11. "Sir Walter Scott," *Spectator*, 24 Sept. 1932, pp. 364 - 65.

12. "Scottish Poetry," *Spectator*, 20 April 1934, p. 625.

13. "Scott and Tradition," *Modern Scot*, 3 (Aug. 1932), 118 - 20.

14. *Scott and Scotland* (London, 1936), pp. 19 - 20. References in the text labeled *SS* are to this edition.

15. *Introductions to English Literature, Volume Five: The Present Age from 1914* (London, 1939), p. 31. References in the text labeled *PA* are to this edition.

16. "Life without Criticism," *Times Literary Supplement*, 24 June 1939, p. 373.

17. " 'Mere Anarchy is Loosed': Literature in a Menaced World," *Times Literary Supplement*, 24 June 1939, p. 377.

18. *Essays on Literature and Society* (London, 1949); "Enlarged and Revised Edition" (London; Cambridge, Mass., 1965), pp. 34 - 35 (American edn.). References in the text labeled *ELS* are to the 1965 American edition.

19. "Laurence Sterne," *Bookman*, 73 (March 1931), 1 - 5.

20. Ibid., p. 1.

21. *Essays on Literature and Society*, p. 158. The latter part of the phrase appears only in the 1949 edition.

22. Edwin Muir, [Review of Harold Osborne, *Aesthetics and Criticism*], *Observer*, 1 May 1955, p. 17.

23. *The Estate of Poetry* (London; Cambridge, Mass., 1962), p. 22. References in the text labeled *EP* are to the American edition.

Chapter Four

1. Edwin Muir, *An Autobiography* (London, 1954), p. 230. References in the text labeled *Auto* are to this volume, which contains almost all of *The Story and the Fable* (London, 1940). Since *An Autobiography* is more easily obtained, I shall refer to it whenever possible.

2. "The Marionette" [review], *Times Literary Supplement*, 19 May 1927, p. 352.

3. *The Marionette* (London, New York, 1927), p. 4. References in the text labeled *M* are to the American edition.

4. *The Three Brothers* (London, New York, 1931), pp. 25 - 26. References in the text labeled *TB* are to the English edn.

5. See the letter to his sister Lizzie, 29 Sept. 1932, *Selected Letters of Edwin Muir*, ed. Peter H. Butter (London, 1974), p. 78.

6. *Poor Tom* (London, 1932), pp. 102 - 104. References in the text labeled *PT* are to this volume.

7. Lawrence Thompson, *Robert Blatchford: Portrait of an Englishman* (London, 1951), p. 130.

8. The main characters in the three novels are linked by similar vowel combinations in their names: *e / e* appears in the feminine names (Gretchen, Ellen, and Helen), while *a / i* (or *ie* or *y*) is found in the male names (Hans, Martin, David, Archie, and Mansie).

9. James Olney, *Metaphors of Self: The Meaning of Autobiography* (Princeton, 1972), pp. 3 - 4.

10. *The Difficult Art of Autobiography* [The Romanes Lecture, 1967] (Oxford, 1968), p. 18.

11. [Review of *An Autobiography*], *New Statesman*, 48 (27 Nov. 1954), 711.

12. "A Question of Tone: Some Problems in Autobiographical Writing," *Essays by Divers Hands, being the Transactions of the Royal Society of Literature*, 33 (1965), 28 - 29.

13. *New Statesman*, 48 (27 Nov. 1954), 711.

14. "Extracts from a Diary, 1937 - 1939," *The Story and the Fable* (London, 1940), p. 263. The passage does not appear in *An Autobiography*.

15. *The Story and the Fable*, p. 235. The passage is extensively revised in *An Autobiography*, p. 193.

Chapter Five

1. These poems, having been first published in different periodicals, were gathered in five collections: *First Poems* (London, New York, 1925); *The Chorus of the Newly Dead* (London, 1926); *Six Poems* (Warlingham, Surrey, 1932); *Variations on a Time Theme* (London, 1934); and *Journeys and Places* (London, 1937). Quotations in this chapter are taken from Edwin Muir, *Collected Poems* (New York, 1965); references in the text labeled *CP* are to this edition. If the poem was not included in this volume, then the quotation is from the appropriate collection as shown by the abbreviations *FP*, *CND*, *SP*, *VTT*, and *JP*.

2. Peter H. Butter, *Edwin Muir* [Writers and Critics Series, ed. A. Norman Jeffares] (Edinburgh, New York, 1962), p. 51. Daniel Hoffman writes with authority on Muir's ballads in his *Barbarous Knowledge: Myth in the Poetry of Yeats, Graves, and Muir* (New York, 1967), pp. 225 - 56.

3. *Bookman*, 61 (Aug. 1925), 703 - 705.

4. Edwin Muir, *An Autobiography* (London, 1954), p. 164.

5. Jolande Jakobi, *The Psychology of C. G. Jung* (New Haven, 1942, 1964), pp. 102, 104.

6. Quoted by Peter H. Butter, *Edwin Muir: Man and Poet* (Edinburgh, 1966), p. 83.

7. *An Autobiography*, p. 206.

8. Ralph J. Mills, Jr., "Edwin Muir's Poetry: An Introductory Note," *Newberry Library Bulletin*, 6 (Nov. 1963), 77.

9. Versions of the poem were published in the *Scottish Chapbook*, 2 (Aug. 1923), 2 - 8, and in the *Calendar of Modern Letters*, 2 (Dec. 1925), 244 - 47.

10. *Selected Letters of Edwin Muir*, ed. Peter H. Butter (London, 1974), p. 37. The letter was written 7 May 1924 from Rosenau, Austria.

11. *An Autobiography*, p. 223.

12. *Edwin Muir: Man and Poet*, p. 104.

13. Only 110 copies were produced, and many of these were destroyed in a fire at the press. Muir included the six poems in *Journeys and Places*, four being given new titles: "Transmutation" became "The Threefold Place"; "The Trance," "The Enchanted Knight"; "Tristram Crazed," "Tristram's Journey"; and "The Field of the Potter," "Judas."

14. The original titles and places of publication are: I. "Interregnum," *Spectator*, 149 (9 Dec. 1932), 827; II. "The Riders," *Listener*, 10 (16 Aug. 1933), 255; III. "Autobiography," *Spectator*, 150 (26 May 1933), 764; VI. "In the Wilderness," *Modern Scot*, 4 (July 1933), 138 - 40; VIII. "The Threefold Time," *New Verse*, No. 6 (Dec. 1933), pp. 3 - 4; IX. "The Dilemma," *Spectator*, 151 (22 Dec. 1933), 932; X. "Heraldry," *Spectator*, 152 (9 March 1934), 375.

15. J. R. Watson, "Edwin Muir and the Problem of Evil," *Critical Quarterly*, 6 (1964), 235.

16. Edwin Muir, "I and Not I," *London Mercury*, 32 (Sept. 1935), 421 - 22.

17. Although this tree image is frequently found in folklore, being associated with myths explaining the creation of the universe (see Mrs. J. H. Philpot, *The Sacred Tree* [London, 1897]), it is also pertinent to note that Muir did not learn the names of trees as a child, there being so few trees in the Orkney Islands, and that Willa Muir, as she once remarked to the present writer, "taught Edwin the names of trees." While this tree-image sprang from his unconscious (its archetypal value is not to be questioned), this connection between trees and his wife must have strengthened its significance to Muir.

18. Graham Greene took the title for his study of Mexico's religious problems in the 1930s, *The Lawless Roads* (London, 1939), from this stanza, also quoting it as an epigraph.

19. The "chapel" and the "castle" are described in *An Autobiography*, pp. 14 - 16.

Chapter Six

1. Edwin Muir, *The Narrow Place* (London, 1943); *The Voyage* (London, 1946). With the exception of "Isaiah" (*The Narrow Place*) and "Dialogue" and "Song" (*The Voyage*), the contents of these volumes are included in Edwin Muir, *Collected Poems* (New York, 1965); and references in the text labeled *CP* are to this volume.

2. Edwin Muir, *An Autobiography* (London, 1954), p. 246.

3. Edwin Muir, "Extracts from a Diary, 1937 - 1939," *The Story and the Fable* (London, 1940), p. 252. This poem is the second of two published in the *London Mercury*, 37 (Nov. 1937), 6 - 7, under the title "Letters I and II." The first poem has not been reprinted.

4. Edwin Muir, *The Present Age from 1914* (London, 1939), p. 43.

5. *An Autobiography*, p. 15.

6. *South Atlantic Quarterly*, 58 (1959), 433.

7. Muir's autobiographical poems parallel the religious paintings of Stanley Spencer (1891 - 1959). The two men were almost exact contemporaries; both had a religious upbringing and, in their early manhood, a prolonged acquaintance with death: Muir in his immediate family circle, Spencer in the first war. But Spencer never lost the order of life that prevailed in his native Cookham and, never "crush[ed] . . . with an iron text," developed much earlier than did Muir.

8. Muir's "A Note on Franz Kafka" in the *Bookman*, 72 (Nov. 1930), 235 - 41, is followed by Conrad Aiken's poem "Prelude" (p. 242). It begins "Thus systole addressed diastole, / The heart contracting, with its grief of burden, / To the lax heart, with grief of burden gone." The similar image and identical diction of Muir's poem are noteworthy.

9. "Extracts from a Diary," *The Story and the Fable*, pp. 252 - 53.

10. In *New Alliance*, 1 (Autumn 1939), 61 - 65, the poem consists of two "Choruses," "The Mother," "The Father," "1st Voice," "2nd Voice," and "3rd Voice," a total of 170 lines. These lines are from the first "Chorus."

11. Muir explains the source of the poem in a letter to Raymond Tschumi, 10 June 1949 (*Selected Letters of Edwin Muir*, ed. Peter H. Butter [London, 1974], pp. 152 - 53); see also Tschumi, *Thought in Twentieth Century English Poetry* (London, 1951), Chapter 2.

12. "Edwin Muir as Poet and Allegorist," *London Magazine*, 7 (March 1960), 48.

13. "The Achievement of Edwin Muir," *Massachusetts Review*, 2 (Winter 1961), 255.

14. One source of this poem may be John Donne's "The Ecstasy": cf. lines 7 - 8, 73 - 74 (*The Complete Poetry of John Donne*, ed. John T. Shawcross [Garden City, N.Y., 1967], pp. 130 - 32).

15. "Edwin Muir as Poet and Allegorist," p. 51.

16. This poem was developed from a story told Muir by Eric Linklater, who recounts the details in a letter to Peter H. Butter quoted in the latter's *Edwin Muir: Man and Poet* (Edinburgh, 1966), pp. 204 - 206. The 1946 version of the poem includes a final stanza omitted from the *Collected Poems:*

> The crowds drew near, the toppling towers;
> In hope and dread we drove to birth;
> The dream and a truth we clutched as ours,
> And gladly, blindly stepped on earth.

17. "Edwin Muir as Poet and Allegorist," p. 52.

Chapter Seven

1. Edwin Muir, *The Labyrinth* (London, 1949); *One Foot in Eden* (London, New York, 1956); *Collected Poems* (London, 1960, 1963; New York, 1965). References in the text labeled *CP* are to the 1965 American edition of the *Collected Poems*. References labeled *OFE* are to *One Foot in Eden*.

2. Christopher Wiseman, "Edwin Muir's 'The Labyrinth': A Study of Symbol and Structure," *Studies in Scottish Literature*, 10 (1972), 73.

3. Elizabeth Huberman, *The Poetry of Edwin Muir: The Field of Good and Ill* (New York, 1971), p. 167.

4. Wiseman, p. 76.

5. "Edwin Muir: *The Journey Back*," *English*, 16 (Autumn 1967), 219.

6. *Barbarous Knowledge: Myth in the Poetry of Yeats, Graves, and Muir* (New York, 1967), pp. 244, 246.

7. Edwin Muir, "The Politics of *King Lear*" [The W. P. Ker Lecture for 1946], *Essays on Literature and Society* (Cambridge, Mass., 1965), pp. 33 - 49.

8. See above, p. 98.

9. Muir explored these ideas in his pamphlet *Social Credit and the Labour Party* (London, 1935), and in his essay "The Natural Man and the Political Man," *Essays on Literature and Society*, pp. 150 - 64.

10. *Edwin Muir: Man and Poet* (Edinburgh, 1966), p. 225.

11. Ibid., p. 300.

12. Ibid., pp. 219, 220.

13. K. L. Goodwin, "Muir's 'The Toy Horse,' " *Explicator*, 23 (1964), Item 6; T. S. K. Scott-Craig, "Muir's 'Toy Horse,' " *Explicator*, 24 (1966), Item 62.

14. Huberman, p. 201.

15. "Edwin Muir and the Problem of Evil," *Critical Quarterly*, 6 (1964), 246.

16. See above, pp. 137 - 38.

17. *Selected Letters of Edwin Muir*, ed. Peter H. Butter (London, 1974), p. 206.

18. Butter reports that in 1954 "Muir explained to . . . a friend at Newbattle . . . that the sense of strain could be lifted by acceptance and prayer" (*Edwin Muir: Man and Poet*, p. 255).

19. See above, pp. 32 - 33.

20. *Twentieth Century Literature*, 12 (July 1966), 99.

21. See above, p. 43.

22. *Edwin Muir: Man and Poet*, p. 256.

23. See above, p. 91.

24. Information from interviews with John Hall; *Selected Letters*, p. 206 (footnote by Peter H. Butter).

25. Willa Muir, *Belonging* (London, 1968), p. 298.

26. Ibid., p. 304.

27. *Selected Letters*, p. 52.

Selected Bibliography

The following list of Edwin Muir's books and of the translations by Willa and Edwin Muir is complete. Muir's many uncollected periodical contributions, including poems, reviews, and essays, as well as his other writings, are listed in *Bibliography of the Writings of Edwin Muir,* by Elgin W. Mellown, University, Alabama: University of Alabama Press, 1964, and in its *Supplement . . . Incorporating Additional Entries,* by Peter Hoy and Elgin W. Mellown, University of Alabama Press, 1970.

The secondary articles listed below have been chosen on the basis of their general helpfulness to the student, who will find a complete listing (to 1970) of such writings, including reviews of Muir's books, in *A Checklist of Writings about Edwin Muir,* by Peter C. Hoy and Elgin W. Mellown, Troy, New York: Whitston Publishing Company, 1971.

PRIMARY SOURCES

1. Books

We Moderns: Enigmas and Guesses. London: George Allen and Unwin, Ltd., 1918; New York: Alfred A. Knopf, 1920. Introduction by H. L. Mencken.

Latitudes. London: Andrew Melrose, Ltd.; New York: B. W. Huebsch, Inc., 1924.

First Poems. London: Hogarth Press; New York: B. W. Huebsch, Inc., 1925.

Chorus of the Newly Dead. London: Hogarth Press, 1926.

Transition. Essays on Contemporary Literature. London: Hogarth Press; New York: Viking Press, 1926.

The Marionette. London: Hogarth Press; New York: Viking Press, 1927.

The Structure of the Novel. London: Hogarth Press, 1928; New York: Harcourt, Brace and Co., 1929.

John Knox: Portrait of a Calvinist. London: Jonathan Cape; New York: Viking Press, 1929.

The Three Brothers. London: William Heinemann, Ltd.; New York: Doubleday, Doran and Co., Inc., 1931.

Six Poems. Warlingham, Surrey: Samson Press, 1932.

Poor Tom. London: J. M. Dent and Sons, Ltd., 1932.

Variations on a Time Theme. London: J. M. Dent and Sons, Ltd., 1934.

Scottish Journey. London: William Heinemann Ltd., in association with Victor Gollancz, Ltd., 1935.

Social Credit and the Labour Party. An Appeal. London: Stanley Nott, Ltd., 1935.

Scott and Scotland. The Predicament of the Scottish Writer. London: George Routledge and Sons, Ltd., 1936; New York: Robert Speller, 1938.

Journeys and Places. London: J. M. Dent and Sons, Ltd., 1937.

The Present Age from 1914. Volume V, Introductions to English Literature, edited by Bonamy Dobrée. London: Cresset Press, 1939; New York: Robert M. McBride and Co., 1940.

The Story and the Fable. An Autobiography. London: George G. Harrap and Co., Ltd., 1940.

The Narrow Place. London: Faber and Faber Ltd., 1943.

The Scots and Their Country. London: Longmans, 1946. No. 8 in the British Council Series, *The British People, How They Live and Work.*

The Voyage and Other Poems. London: Faber and Faber Ltd., 1946.

The Politics of King Lear. Glasgow: Jackson, Son and Co., 1947. The W. P. Memorial Lecture, University of Glasgow, 1946.

Essays on Literature and Society. London: Hogarth Press, 1949. Enlarged and Revised Edition, London: Hogarth Press; Cambridge, Mass.: Harvard University Press, 1965.

The Labyrinth. London: Faber and Faber Ltd., 1949.

Collected Poems, 1921 - 1951. London: Faber and Faber Ltd., 1952; New York: Grove Press, 1953. Introduction by John C. Hall, editor.

Prometheus. London: Faber and Faber Ltd., 1954. An Ariel Poem, illustrated by John Piper.

An Autobiography. London: Hogarth Press; New York: William Sloane Associates, Inc., 1954. Paperback edition, London: Methuen University Paperbacks, 1964.

One Foot in Eden. London: Faber and Faber Ltd.; New York: Grove Press, 1956.

Collected Poems, 1921 - 1958. London: Faber and Faber Ltd., 1960. *Collected Poems.* London: Faber and Faber Ltd., 1963. *Collected Poems.* New York: Oxford University Press, 1965. Preface by T. S. Eliot.

The Estate of Poetry. London: Hogarth Press; Cambridge, Mass.: Harvard University Press, 1962. Foreword by Archibald MacLeish.

Selected Poems. London: Faber and Faber Ltd., 1965. Preface by T. S. Eliot.

Selected Letters of Edwin Muir. London: Hogarth Press, 1974. Edited and introduced by Peter H. Butter.

2. Translations by Willa and Edwin Muir
Asch, Sholem. *Three Cities.* London: Gollancz; New York: Putnam, 1933.

_____. *Salvation*. London: Gollancz; New York: Putnam, 1934.

_____. *Mottke the Thief*. London: Gollancz; New York: Putnam, 1935.

_____. *Calf of Paper*. London: Gollancz; New York: Putnam, 1936. American title: *War Goes On*.

Broch, Hermann. *The Sleepwalkers*. London: Martin Secker; New York: Little, 1932.

_____. *The Unknown Quantity*. London: Collins; New York: Viking Press, 1935.

Burckhardt, Carl Jakob. *Richelieu*. London: George Allen and Unwin; New York: Nelson, 1940. Revision edited by Charles H. Carter, New York: Vintage Books (Random House), 1964.

Feuchtwanger, Lion. *Jew Süss*. London: Martin Secker; New York: Viking Press, 1926. American title: *Power*.

_____. *The Ugly Duchess*. London: Martin Secker, 1927; New York: Viking Press, 1928.

_____. *Two Anglo-Saxon Plays: The Oil Islands* and *Warren Hastings*. London: Martin Secker, 1929; New York: Viking Press, 1928.

_____. *Success*. London: Martin Secker; New York: Viking Press, 1930.

_____. *Josephus*. London: Martin Secker; New York: Viking Press, 1932.

_____. *The Jew of Rome*. London: Hutchinson, 1935; New York: Viking Press, 1936.

_____. *False Nero*. London: Hutchinson; New York: Viking Press, 1937. American title: *Pretender*.

Glaeser, Ernst. *Class of 1902*. London: Martin Secker; New York: Viking Press, 1929.

Harsányi, Zsolt. *Through the Eyes of a Woman*. London: Routledge, 1941. New York: Putnam, 1940. American title: *Through a Woman's Eyes*.

_____. *Lover of Life*. New York: Putnam, 1942. Translated in collaboration with Paul Tabor.

Hauptmann, Gerhart. *Poetic Dramas (Indipohdi, The White Saviour,* and *A Winter Ballad)*. London: Martin Secker; New York: B. W. Huebsch, Inc., 1925.

_____. *The Island of the Great Mother*. London: Martin Secker; New York: Viking Press, 1925.

_____. *Historic and Legendary Dramas (Veland)*. London: Martin Secker; New York: Viking Press, 1929.

Heuser, Kurt. *Inner Journey*. London: Martin Secker; New York: Viking Press, 1932. American title: *Journey Inward*.

Kafka, Franz. *The Castle*. London: Martin Secker; New York: Knopf, 1930.

_____. *The Great Wall of China and Other Pieces*. London: Martin Secker, 1933; New York: Schocken, 1946. American title: *The Great Wall of China Stories and Reflections*.

_____. *The Trial*. London: Gollancz; New York: Knopf, 1937.

_____. *America*. London: Routledge, 1938; New York: New Directions, 1940.

_____. *Parables, in German and English.* New York: Schocken, 1947. Part of this work was translated by Clement Greenberg.

_____. *In the Penal Settlement. Tales and Short Pieces.* London: Martin Secker; New York: Schocken, 1948.

Kühnelt-Leddihn, Erik Maria von. *Night over the East.* London: Sheed and Ward; New York: Oxford University Press, 1936.

Lothar, Ernst. *Little Friend.* London: Martin Secker; New York: Putnam, 1933.

_____. *The Mills of God.* London: Martin Secker; New York: Putnam, 1935. American title: *The Loom of Justice.*

Mann, Heinrich. *Hill of Lies.* London: Jarrolds, 1934; New York: Dutton, 1935.

Neumann, Robert. *The Queen's Doctor.* London: Gollancz; New York: Knopf, 1936.

_____. *A Woman Screamed.* London: Cassell; New York: Dial Press, 1938. Revision entitled *Failure of a Hero.* London: Hutchinson's Universal Book Club, 1948.

Paléologue, Georges Maurice. *Enigmatic Czar.* London: Hamilton; New York: Harper, 1938.

Renn, Ludwig [Arnold Friedrich, Vieth von Golssenau]. *War.* London: Martin Secker; New York: Dodd, 1929.

_____. *After War.* London: Martin Secker; New York: Dodd, 1931.

Rheinhardt, Emil Alphons. *The Life of Eleanora Duse.* London: Martin Secker, 1930.

SECONDARY SOURCES

AITCHISON, JAMES. "The Limits of Experience: Edwin Muir's 'Ballad of the Soul,' " *English*, 24 (1975), 10 - 15. A study of this early poem from the Jungian point of view which Maurice Nicoll is presumed to have taught Muir.

BLACKMUR, R. P. "Edwin Muir: Between the Tiger's Paws," in Don C. Allen, editor, *Four Poets on Poetry.* Baltimore: Johns Hopkins Press, 1959, pp. 24 - 43. An appreciative consideration of the traditional qualities in Muir's poems.

BUTTER, PETER H. *Edwin Muir* [Writers and Critics Series]. Edinburgh: Oliver and Boyd; New York: Grove Press, 1962. An introductory survey of Muir's writings.

_____. *Edwin Muir: Man and Poet.* Edinburgh: Oliver and Boyd, 1966. The authorized biography; also contains previously unpublished diary entries and letters by Muir and extensive criticism of his writings.

_____. "Edwin Muir: *The Journey Back,*" *English,* 16 (1967), 218 - 22. A close study of Muir's longest poem, emphasizing its religious meaning.

COX, C. B., and A. E. DYSON. *Modern Poetry: Studies in Practical Criticism.* London: Edward Arnold (Publishers) Ltd., 1963, pp. 128 - 32. An accurate if somewhat simplistic analysis of "The Horses."

GARBER, FREDRICK. "Edwin Muir's Heraldic Mode," *Twentieth Century Literature*, 12 (July 1966), 96 - 103. A study of the heraldic images and of the larger implications of these images.

GLICKSBURG, CHARLES I. "Edwin Muir: Zarathustra in Scotch Dress," *Arizona Quarterly*, 12 (1956), 225 - 39. A summary and discussion of Muir's Nietzschean attitudes in the pre-1929 books; otherwise valid generalizations must be qualified by failure to acknowledge periodical contributions and other writings.

HALL, JOHN C. *Edwin Muir* [British Council Writers and Their Work Series No. 71]. London: Longmans, Green and Co., 1956. An early but still valuable introduction to Muir's work.

HAMBURGER, MICHAEL. "Edwin Muir," *Encounter*, 15 (Dec. 1960), 46 - 53. Reprinted in Hamburger's *Art as Second Nature. Occasional Pieces, 1950 - 74*. Cheadle Hulme, Cheshire: Carcanet New Press Ltd., 1975, pp. 86 - 102. A convincing delineation of Muir the man and review of the *Collected Poems* in the light of the poet's personal qualities.

HASSAN, IHAB. "Of Time and Emblematic Reconciliation: Notes on the Poetry of Edwin Muir," *South Atlantic Quarterly*, 58 (1959), 427 - 39. A still valuable early recognition of Muir's concern with time and of the poetic techniques through which the time theme is treated.

HOFFMAN, DANIEL. *Barbarous Knowledge: Myth in the Poetry of Yeats, Graves, and Muir*. New York: Oxford University Press, 1967, pp. 225 - 56. A short, authoritative study within the context of a larger exploration of myth, folklore, and dreams.

HOLLOWAY, JOHN. "The Poetry of Edwin Muir," *Hudson Review*, 13 (1960 - 1961), 550 - 67. An important evaluation of the poems: "the foundation of Muir's achievement . . . is not a voguish manipulation of language, but the embodiment in verse of a deep and true apprehension of life" (p. 557).

HUBERMAN, ELIZABETH. *The Poetry of Edwin Muir. The Field of Good and Ill*. New York: Oxford University Press, 1971. An intense, close study of the poems, stressing their musical qualities and Muir's humanism.

JENNINGS, ELIZABETH. "Edwin Muir as Poet and Allegorist," *London Magazine*, 7 (March 1960), 43 - 56. A well-balanced, convincing general study of the poems, emphasizing Muir's Christian faith.

KEEBLE, BRIAN. "In Time's Despite: On the Poetry of Edwin Muir," *Sewanee Review*, 81 (1973), 633 - 58; "Edwin Muir: Our Contemporary and Mentor," *Agenda*, 12, iv - 13, i (1975), 79 - 87. Examination of the poems with emphasis on the religious and philosophical themes and placing of Muir as a poet loyal to "the timeless Truth of the perennial Tradition."

MILLS, RALPH J., JR. "Eden's Gate: The Later Poetry of Edwin Muir," *Personalist*, 44 (1963), 58 - 78. A valuable general appreciation of *One Foot in Eden* and *Collected Poems* as the work of a traditional, religious visionary; by one of Muir's most understanding critics.

MORGAN, EDWIN. "Edwin Muir," *The Review*, No. 5 (Feb. 1963), pp. 3 -

10. A balanced, discriminating evaluation of Muir's attitude in the postwar poems.

MORGAN, KATHLEEN E. *Christian Themes in Contemporary Poets: A Study of English Poetry in the Twentieth Century*. London: SCM Press Ltd., 1965. "The Search for a Pattern: Poetry of Edwin Muir," pp. 43 - 57. A convincing study of the poems (within the context of a consideration of Christianity in modern poetry) that shows Muir's development of a coherent, religious interpretation of life.

MUIR, WILLA. *Belonging: A Memoir*. London: Hogarth Press, 1968. A parallel account by the poet's widow of many of the events described in *An Autobiography*.

RAINE, KATHLEEN. *Defending Ancient Springs*. London: Oxford University Press, 1967. "Edwin Muir," pp. 1 - 16. Sensitive appreciation of Muir as a symbolist poet in the Blake-Yeats tradition by his friend and fellow poet who has written a number of other important studies of his work.

SCHOLTEN, MARTIN. "The Humanism of Edwin Muir," *College English*, 21 (1960), 322 - 26. A description of the distinguishing characteristics of Muir's humanistic philosophy.

SUMMERS, JOSEPH H. "The Achievement of Edwin Muir," *Massachusetts Review*, 2 (1961), 240 - 60. An introductory survey of the prose and poetry, stressing the major themes and interests.

WATSON, J. R. "Edwin Muir and the Problem of Evil," *Critical Quarterly*, 6 (1964), 231 - 49. A well-reasoned general study of the poems as they illustrate Muir's handling of the concept of evil.

WISEMAN, CHRISTOPHER. "Edwin Muir's 'The Labyrinth': A Study of Symbol and Structure," *Studies in Scottish Literature*, 10 (1972), 67 - 78; "A Study of Edwin Muir's "The Horses,'" *Scottish Literary Journal*, 1 (1974), 39 - 49; "Edwin Muir's Last Poems," *University of Windsor Review*, 10, i (1974), 5 - 20. Valuable close readings of the indicated poems.

Index

177

828.912
m953

107 757